BROCK PETERS
MEMORIAL

FOR SOME OF US THE WORLD WILL BE
FRACTIONALLY IMBALANCED FOR A LITTLE WHILE.
THEN IT WILL CORRECT ITSELF, AS IT ALWAYS HAS.

IN THE PROCESS--AS ALWAYS--FAMILY MEMBERS,
FRIENDS-
ACQUAINTANCES-
AND ADMIRERERS-

WILL FACE THE MANY DIFFICULT, BUT NECESSARY,
ADJUSTMENTS THAT INEVITABLY ARISE-
WHEN SOMEONE SO LOVED, SO RESPECTED, SO
ADMIRED GOES AWAY.

BUT- OUR RESTORATIVE POWERS-
LIKE THE *That of the* WORLD'S-
WILL KICK IN--AND WE WILL

EEDED

THIRT
A MI

ONWARD STILL. A BILLION YEARS. 15 BI
AT THE SPEED OF 186,000 MILES PER SECO
ETERNITY BEYOND. BUT, GOD HAS YET TO M
THAT WASN'T UP TO THE DISTANCE. MY
MADE IT. MY FATHER, BROTHERS AND SIST
AND RESPECTED ACQUAINTANCES. AND N
WINDT -- HUSBAND, FATHER, LOVED ONE,
RESPECTED ACQUAINTANCE HAS ALSO ARR
ALREADY THERE. DON'T TRY TO CALCULATE T
COVERED. THOSE NUMBERS ARE ONLY USEFUL
MATERIAL WORLD. OVER THERE, GOD HAS S
GET HIS SPIRITS HOME.

SO, SUZANNE AND TRACY, BE AT EASE IN
AND IN YOUR HEARTS. LET YOUR GRIEF FACE
OPEN YOURSELVES TO AS FULL AND MEANINGF
YOU CAN POSSIBLY HAVE.

AMONG THE STARS -- NOT O
HEAVENS AS WELL.

CCOMP
OM LIF
IN M
STION
HEN A
NCE S
V.
F HAL
ARABLE
O OF
HIS SI
R - SUC
HEART
TO ETE
CAL UN
ST TO

F LIG
HIRTY THOUSAND
PIRITS INFINITELY

s a long, lonely line, daily.

efeat.

ngs us to moments like these,

ctive "thank-you" is loudly

dest tools—

by inch—

life.

s, barely managed to
destly.

ere insufficient to the task--

vas Richard Pryor—

the rest of us.

a great talent—

ish smile—

MAKE THE MANY DIFFICULT AJUSTMENTS
NECESSARY TO HOLD THE LIFE OF ~~THE DEPARTED~~ *A Christine Smith*
~~LOVED ONE~~ IN OUR EMBRACE FOREVER.
*Who was This Departed Loved one For whom we have
Gathered here Today a Final Goodby* WHO IS THIS, THIS
*she was many
Things To most of us, a grandmother or a mother, her son, a wife
To her Husband, grandmother To her grandchildren, A* WHO IS THIS ACTOR, THIS SINGER, THIS
PRODUCER, ~~THIS LECTURER,~~ THIS DOER OF GOOD
who constantly tried to ~~lessen~~ lighten the burdens of life ~~on~~ the whenever
NAMED BROCK PETERS! *they fall on the backs of
Family members, Friends or neighbors*
SIXTY YEARS AGO, BROCK PETERS, WILLIAM
GREAVES, EARL HYMAN, CHARLIE BLACKWELL,
WILLIAM MARSHALL, JULIAN MAYFIELD, JAMES
EDWARDS, THE INCOMPARABLE ROSCO LEE BROWN,
IVAN DIXON AND MYSELF—
EACH HAD CHOSEN TO BECOME ACTORS IN THE
AMERICAN THEATRE.

SOME OF US BECAME WRITERS INSTEAD, SOME OF
US BECAME DIRECTORS INSTEAD, SOME OF US
DIDN'T MAKE IT. THE LUCK OF THE DRAW
EVENTUALLY TURNED THEIR INTERESTS TO OTHER

---

ultimately, demolish the man, b

n forty years.

a need on the part of such a

as a threat instead of as a gift

astounding. Of all the educate

science, technology, the legal

ts necessary to develop and k

here was no room for this accor

credentials, an exceptional intell

his culture and his people. Th

te this extraordinary human bei

brought with him the color of h

SIDNEY POITIER

SIDNEY POITIER

THE GREAT SPEECHES OF AN ICON WHO MOVED US FORWARD

Sidney Poitier
with **Joanna Poitier**

Edited by JOHN MALAHY

Foreword by OPRAH WINFREY

RUNNING PRESS
PHILADELPHIA

Running Press
Hachette Book Group
1290 Avenue of the Americas, New York, NY 10104
www.runningpress.com
@Running_Press

First Edition: October 2024

Published by Running Press, an imprint of Hachette Book Group, Inc.
The Running Press name and logo are trademarks of Hachette Book Group, Inc.

The Hachette Speakers Bureau provides a wide range of authors for speaking events. To find out more, go to
www.hachettespeakersbureau.com or email HachetteSpeakers@hbgusa.com.

Running Press books may be purchased in bulk for business, educational, or promotional use. For more information, please
contact your local bookseller or the Hachette Book Group Special Markets Department at Special.Markets@hbgusa.com.

The publisher is not responsible for websites (or their content) that are not owned by the publisher.

Print book cover and interior design by Susan Van Horn
Photo Credits: Page 14: MediaPunch Inc / Alamy Stock Photo. Pages 23, 31, 36, 80, 83, 85, 87, 91, 95, 96, 145, 153, 156: Photofest.
Page 49 © Republic Pictures / Everett Collection. Page 88: Everett Collection. Page 118: © AP Photo/Clark Jones.
All other photographs from the Sidney Poitier Estate.

Library of Congress Cataloging-in-Publication Data

Names: Poitier, Sidney, author. | Shimkus, Joanna, 1943– author.
Title: Sidney Poitier : the great speeches of an icon who moved us forward
   / Sidney Poitier, with Joanna Poitier.
Description: First edition. | Philadelphia : Running Press, 2024. |
   Includes index. | Summary: "From the Poitier estate, the words of film
   legend and cultural icon Sidney Poitier come to life in his wise, witty,
   inspiring, and deeply personal speeches on entertainment history,
   culture, civil rights, and more" —Provided by publisher.
Identifiers: LCCN 2023044381 (print) | LCCN 2023044382 (ebook) | ISBN
   9780762487172 (hardcover) | ISBN 9780762487196 (ebook)
Subjects: LCSH: Poitier, Sidney. | Speeches, addresses, etc.,
   American—African American authors. | Actors—United States—Biography.
   | African American actors—Biography.
Classification: LCC PN2287.P57 A5 2024 (print) | LCC PN2287.P57 (ebook) |
   DDC 791.4302/809273 [B] —dc23/eng/20240102
LC record available at https://lccn.loc.gov/2023044381
LC ebook record available at https://lccn.loc.gov/2023044382

ISBNs: 978-0-7624-8717-2 (hardcover), 978-0-7624-8719-6 (ebook)
Printed in China
RRD-APS

10 9 8 7 6 5 4 3 2 1

To all readers of this book, with you

I share Sidney's favorite quote:

May the wind be at your back for all

your endeavors, and may all that

you wish for happen, always.

CONTENTS

FOREWORD

I miss our Sunday calls. For years, Sidney Poitier and I would spend hours in discourse about all things great and small. His daughters taking him shopping to upgrade his wardrobe. Why he never used the word God but preferred "The Forces" instead.

How integrity shows up best when everything else has fallen apart. This was truly an amazement to me, who grew up not even daring to dream I'd someday meet him.

That I, in my lifetime, got to truly know him, and he so fully know me, is one of the greatest blessings of my life.

He was, as Toni Morrison describes of a character in *Beloved*, "a friend to mind." Every encounter I experienced with him, I walked

away more enhanced, enlivened, and more in touch with myself and values that matter.

It's no surprise that the care and curiosity given to me and everyone he met is evident in how he approached his public speaking. He didn't hire speech writers—he labored with his own self-teaching to come up with just the right articulation to express not only his sentiments but to let us see in many ways how he saw himself. He personified eloquence, integrity, and Grace.

He not only earned our respect, he commanded it. Always a powerful symbol of courage, Sidney Poitier broke through social barriers from the moment he set foot in Hollywood. Every character he played had something important to say.

And here, in his own words, we get to hear about some of what he considered worthy of giving voice to.

I often wish that I had recorded (with his permission) many of our Sunday calls.

I would have taken all those delightful and often funny exchanges and compiled a book of lessons called *Sundays with Sidney*.

The notes I hurriedly scribbled during our conversations were not extensive enough to write a book. But fortunately for us, he kept his own speeches, and now we have forever a glimpse at his wisdom, his wit, his grace, his words.

Oprah Winfrey

A NOTE FROM JOANNA POITIER

The first time I saw Sidney in person, I had been asked by a film director to fly to Los Angeles and meet the leading man of his upcoming movie—"the great Sidney Poitier." When I met him, I recall he was wearing a pale blue suit with an ascot. I wasn't sure what to make of that. But he was very sweet, we had lunch and talked, and though I had made it clear I wasn't interested in doing a screen test, the producers liked me and I got the job.

The next time I saw him was in Paris, where I had been living and working for several years. At the time I was engaged to an Englishman, so when Sidney showed up that summer, we simply spent time together as friends. He asked me to take him to the Louvre, but when I arrived at his hotel, La Trémoille, I found him still in his pajamas. Maybe he wasn't the best at first impressions. He explained that he had overslept and invited me into his room to have lunch. I stayed, and we talked and talked. As I was leaving, he asked, "Did anyone ever say you have childbearing hips?" I thought, *No, thank you.* (That's the worst thing you can say to a woman.) But we wound up going to the Louvre the next day.

At Sidney's 70th birthday celebration in 1997

It wasn't until the filming of *The Lost Man* in Philadelphia that fall that I knew he was the one—and we were together for over fifty years.

Sidney was really an amazing person, and the most interesting and intellectual man that I've ever known—and I've known quite a few. He was a freak about the cosmos, and

he and Carl Sagan had a very nice relationship. Sidney was so intelligent, especially knowing that he only had two or three years of schooling and was totally self-taught. He was a special, unique guy. I don't know why he picked me.

He was also prolific in his writing, an amazing thinker and speaker. In the last few years, I have been going through his many speeches. They are inspiring and full of wisdom, and I think other people should be able to enjoy them, too.

Reading through his words, it becomes clear that the most important thing for Sidney—beyond his family—was education. What he wanted most in life was for his children to be educated, probably because he never really had a formal education himself. He set up a trust for his daughters to go to college, and of course he publicly supported the great work of organizations like the United Negro College Fund and the Fulfillment Fund.

Sidney had the most soothing, relaxing, loving voice. He spoke very deliberately—a result of mimicking radio hosts when he was trying to break into acting in New York. His tone was so unique, not a typical American accent, not really Bahamian. Although we lived in the Bahamas for several years

after we were married, I never heard his original accent. I never heard him raise his voice either, even with the children, and I know that he and I never really had any arguments.

Today I feel protective of Sidney's legacy, in part because he was very protective of it and very particular about doing any project. He would never do something just for the money—commercials, sponsorships, whatever. He wasn't interested in making a ton of money. But he would agree to work on a film if he was impressed with the filmmaker's work. In this way he was a very simple, genuine, honest human being. And very caring of everybody.

In short, he was the most wonderful man I have ever known—who was also the best father, most loving husband, and my best friend.

Sidney—I will always love you, beyond forever.

Your Joanna

OPPOSITE: **At a party in 2007**

INTRODUCTION

Sidney Poitier looms large in film history. This is no doubt due to his indelible screen presence and his ability to command our fullest attention, thrill us with his delivery, charm us with his charisma, and rally us in support of his determined heroes. But it is also a result of the symbolism of "Sidney Poitier," that rarest of things: a Black leading man in the days of the film industry's nascent stumbling in the direction of racial equality, in an America on the cusp of truer democracy.

Hollywood's Sidney Poitier struck the nation like lightning. But his roles in films like *The Defiant Ones*, *Guess Who's Coming to Dinner*, *In the Heat of the Night*, *To Sir, with Love*, and *A Patch of Blue* were largely symbolic. Most of the time, he was asked to play characters who were certain of their beliefs, preternaturally wise, morally honorable, resolved, unwavering. Through his movie roles, he spoke multiracial truths to monoracial power structures. The stereotype of Black integrity would become his persona.

The words he is best known for—"They call me Mr. Tibbs"—while powerful and memorable, are not *his* words. They are those of a

scriptwriter—Stirling Silliphant—who took them verbatim from the author of the novel *In the Heat of the Night*—John Ball—that were approved by a studio and fashioned by a director, their specific tone selected by an editor, the whole package released to the public by exhibitors. The statement is terse, defiant, righteous, and—half a century later—it still packs a punch.

When Sidney spoke publicly, he spoke slowly. He enunciated with care—as if he were practicing the words in his head, mulling them over, chewing each syllable in his mouth before delivering it, with purpose, into the world. And what power lay behind those syllables. His voice is consistently warm of tone, sure of itself, purposeful, and true, and it echoes in the mind of audiences.

"I've always believed that my work should convey my personal values," Sidney writes in the introduction to his 2000 autobiography, *The Measure of a Man*. This is no less true for his public addresses than it is for his performances and directorial work, his authorship and political activism.

The speeches contained in this book are proof. The words are Sidney's own. They are unfiltered and authentic, but no less eloquent than those of his scriptwriters. And except for some judicious trimming here and there, they are unedited and exactly how Sidney intended them to be.

In an origin story told often in his public addresses, Sidney was born in Miami, Florida, to a family of Bahamian tomato farmers. After returning to the United States as a teenager—largely uneducated, working meager jobs as a young African American in the 1940s while trying to break into acting—he learned to read with the help of a kind Jewish waiter. Aware that his Bahamian accent was a liability on Broadway, he diligently practiced it away by mimicking the articulate tones of radio host Norman Brokenshire. The new voice had no exotic Caribbean quality and little hint of the inner city, which doubtlessly helped endear Sidney to a white mainstream audience.

He became a success on Broadway and soon also in Hollywood, where his manner and voice were tailor-made for a postwar industry that was unafraid to go on the offense with regard to civil rights. And he thrived, as well as a Black movie icon could thrive in the 1950s and '60s. "Sidney Poitier has been one of the best reasons for going to the movies these last two decades," critic Pauline Kael wrote in 1969.

At the same time, he endured a lot of criticism for essentially being a singular Black individual who—thanks in no part to his own decisions—was made by white Hollywood to stand in for an entire race in a series of mainstream social-problem pictures, rather than diversifying either the talent pool or the content of acting roles. Hollywood lacked the will or the imagination for more than a decade to hire other Black actors or offer up complex roles for a Black audience—doors that Sidney would ironically help open. "Why does white America love Sidney Poitier so?" asked the *New York Times*, cynically, in 1967. Perhaps it is because Hollywood didn't give them other options, didn't have the

guts to, and didn't possess the confident tenacity of a Sidney Poitier.

Later in his life he would become an author, in more than one sense—first as director of several feature films, beginning with 1972's *Buck and the Preacher*, and later as a writer of both autobiographies and a novel, 2013's *Montaro Caine*. In his bestselling memoir *This Life* (1980) and his later "spiritual autobiography," *The Measure of a Man*, he laid out the case for himself as a humble but proud actor, a dedicated husband and father. He won a Grammy Award for Best Spoken Word Album in 2001 for *The Measure of a Man* and earned a second nomination for *Life beyond Measure: Letters to My Great-Granddaughter* (2008).

And of course, he was invited to speak. He spoke publicly not just to accept life achievement awards but to honor artistic and cultural organizations with his presence and his tacit endorsement, and to regale them with his decades of earned wisdom.

His themes varied based on the circumstance, and that is for the most part how this book is organized. A curious student of the cosmos and big scientific questions, he spoke often about the concept of human evolution—in both literal and artistic senses. He talked about primordial soup to a Dallas Center for the Performing Arts audience and about cave dwellers and hunter-gatherers to the Detroit Institute of Arts. With these thoughts, he constructed an allegory on the creation of art, paired with the belief that we stand on the shoulders of those who come before us and, together, create a path forward.

He preached the importance of struggle, both for one's own development and for society. He reiterated the need for family and tradition, for honoring one's parents and passing down wisdom to one's children. A self-taught man, he cared passionately about education and student opportunity. He was also an optimist, sure that our best days are ahead of us because he recognized steady improvements in our world and the inherent goodness of people in it.

In memorial speeches and industry tributes, he spoke especially eloquently about his friends and colleagues. And he had a knack for getting to the heart of the matter. About Dorothy Dandridge, he wrote "she was more of a star than the circumstances of her time could make room for." It would be hard to state her case in a more succinct or bittersweet fashion. Upon death of Hollywood agent Freddie Fields, he said, "For some of us the world will be fractionally imbalanced for a little while. Then it will correct itself, as it always has." It may be helpful to think about Sidney, who passed away in 2022, in a similar way.

These speeches were pulled directly from Sidney's own files. Where possible, they were checked against recordings and official records—many are available for viewing online, and some have been transcribed or quoted in the press. In several cases, the written versions kept in Sidney's files conflict with the final ones presented. In such circumstances, we have deferred to the delivered speech in structure, but not necessarily in content. We have endeavored to present Sidney's most complete version of a given speech, even if it was not ultimately delivered as such, for reasons of timing or otherwise. In so doing, we hope to honor his full intentions. It is important to remember that words on a page aren't necessarily the words spoken aloud when one gives a speech. While this is clear enough when comparing written notes against a recording, it must also be assumed about the speeches that were *not* recorded.

Reading a speech is akin to reading a play. A reader can get the gist, but not the force of expression delivered by a gifted speaker. In this case the speaker was a master of his craft, and his voice continues to echo. When Sidney spoke, he spoke for many. He was a true screen hero—or, as he might put it, a carrier of other people's dreams.

SP: Remarks for Academy
2002

I arrived in Hollywood at the age of 22. In a time
different than today's. A time in which the odds against
my standing here tonight, fifty three years later, would not
have fallen in my favor. Back then no route had been
established for where I was hoping to go. No pathway
left in evidence for me to trace. No custom for me to
follow.

Yet, here I am this evening at the end of a journey that, in
1949 would have been considered close to impossible –
and, in fact might never have been set in motion; were
there not – an untold number of courageous, unselfish
choices made by a handful of visionary film makers –
directors, writers, producers – each with a strong sense of
citizenship responsibility to the times in which they lived.
Each unafraid to permit their art to reflect their views and
values – ethical and moral –and, moreover, acknowledge
them as their own; even as they faced the mindset that
was guarding the gates of uncharted territories--they knew
the odds that stood against them were overwhelming;
odds that could prove themselves too high to overcome.
Still they persevered. And I benefited from their efforts,
the industry benefited from their effort, America benefited
from their effort, and, in ways large and small, the world
has also benefited from their effort.

Therefore, with respect--I share this great honor with:

Stanley Kramer, Joe Mankewitz, Darrel Zanuk, The
Mirisch Brothers, Guy Green, Norman Jewison – and the
host of others who have had a hand in making this
moment possible. My love and my thanks to my
wonderful wife Joanna, my children, my grandchildren
and my agent and friend, Martin Baum--one of the good
guys. Thank you.

[handwritten annotations:] have; speaking through their art to the best in all of; THE LATE THE LATE THE LATE; ESPECIALLY WALTER; ALTERING THE ODDS. WITHOUT; would their work and other values have spoken to the; MOST would not have come to pass; inaue

[handwritten note:] To the PEOPLE ARRound
THE WORLD WHO HAVE PLACED
THEIR TRUST IN MY JUDGMENT
AS AN ACTOR AND FILMMAKER
thank you all For your
Support. Through The Years

LADIES AND GENTLEMEN —
I AM DELIGHTED TO BE HERE.

MY THANKS —
AND DEEPEST APPRECIATION —

TO THOSE WHOSE HEARTS AND
MINDS —
HAVE MADE THIS
EXTRAORDINARY EVENING
POSSIBLE.

THE HEARTS AND MINDS —
OF MEN AND WOMEN WHOSE
DAILY EXISTENCE —
ENRICHES, COMPLIMENTS, AND
REINFORCES THE DIGNITY OF
HUMAN LIFE.

IN A PROCESS
THAT IS EVER ONGOING —

SUCH ARE THE HEARTS AND MINDS —
THAT HAVE SO GRACIOUSLY
INVITED ME —
TO COME — AND BE RECEIVED —

AS THIS EVENINGS HONOREE —

IF I HAVE INDEED
MANAGED TO
REFLECT —

IN SOME SMALL MEASURE, AT LEAST A FEW, O
THE VALUES AND PRINCIPLES —

THAT ARE THE VERY
FOUNDATION —

ON WHICH THIS RESPECTED AND
CELEBRATED MARIAN
ANDERSON AWARD SO PROUDLY
SITS.

THEN, LADIES AND GENTLEMEN —

I ACCEPT THIS AWARD WITH THE FULL KNOWL
THAT IT WILL REQUIRE MY VERY BEST EFFORT

TO BALANCE WITH GRACE —

THIS MOST DISTINGUISHED HONOR YOU HAVE
UPON MY
UNWORTHY HEAD —

TO WEAR IT WELL, MY REACH
MUST CONSTANTLY EXCEED MY
GRASP.

WITH SUCH A TASK AHEAD —
LET ME BEGIN BY TAKING FIRST
THINGS FIRST.

I — LIKE ALL HONOREES
WHO HAVE PRECEDED ME —

MAJOR HONORS AND AWARDS

Thank you all for having helped mine to be
one hell of a journey.

Sidney Poitier had an inauspicious early life. Raised on Cat Island in the Bahamas in the 1920s and '30s, he was—from an American perspective, and certainly from a Hollywood one—disadvantaged with the wrong childhood environment, skin color, and accent, but nevertheless he was destined to help change the world's most powerful country and one of its most influential industries—the movies—forever.

Consider his story: largely self-educated, through his own determination and struggle, he became a celebrated stage actor in New York before being plucked up by producers for a starring role in the movies. His lucky timing included a postwar climate of racial openness and a studio appetite for tackling social problems on-screen. With his adopted American accent, he was able to speak directly to millions of Americans, softening hearts and humbling attitudes in the process, and he remains an icon for generations of moviegoers.

Given his legacy, he was an obvious candidate for lifetime achievement awards inside and outside the industry in his later years. In addition to the honors listed in this chapter, he received the Cecil B. DeMille Award from the Hollywood Foreign Press Association in 1982, a Kennedy Center Honor in 1995, the Life Achievement Award from the Screen Actors Guild in 2000, a British Academy of Film and Television Arts (BAFTA) Fellowship in 2016, and many more.

OPPOSITE: Sidney won the Academy Award for Best Actor on April 13, 1964, for his work in *Lilies of the Field*, a low-budget drama that became a critical and commercial hit. He was the first African American to win a lead acting Oscar, a watershed in the history of Hollywood.

AFI LIFE ACHIEVEMENT AWARD

March 12, 1992
Los Angeles, California

The "AFI Salute to Sidney Poitier," the twentieth such ceremony honoring the life of a major Hollywood figure by the American Film Institute, was hosted by Sidney's close friend and colleague Harry Belafonte. The AFI Life Achievement Award is given annually to a member of the film community who has "in a fundamental way advanced the art of film and whose work had stood the test of time." The night was one of the most memorable professional events of Sidney's life, not in the least because of the attendance of his family, including his six daughters and one granddaughter.

Tributes were given by Denzel Washington, Danny Glover, Richard Widmark, Tony Curtis, Stanley Kramer, Lee Grant, Morgan Freeman, John Singleton, Rod Steiger, James Earl Jones, and Louis Gossett Jr. Additional attendees included civil rights icon Rosa Parks, who received a standing ovation. AFI founder and chairman George Stevens Jr.–who had directed Sidney in the 1991 miniseries *Separate but Equal*–presented Sidney with the award. The event was filmed and later televised nationally on NBC.

As would often be the case, his speech mentions not only the influential colleagues of his career–including director Joseph L. Mankiewicz, who launched Sidney's film career with *No Way Out* (1950)–but also old friends, like Yorick Rolle from his childhood in the Bahamas. Later, he symbolically passes the torch to a new generation of African American filmmakers.

I fully expected to be wise by now. I missed. I have come to this place in my life armed only with the knowledge of how little I know. I never expected that. For much of my youth I looked, but I couldn't see. Now I have arrived at a point where I can sometimes see without looking. I never expected that.

As a young man, when I first got to know the world and where I was situated in it, I developed a strong belief that the time would change. Now, it is clear, that I am changed by time. I never expected that.

I have carried a cherished secret in my bosom for, now, some thirty years or more—the deeply held conviction that I can sing songs as well and tell stories as funnily as Harry Belafonte and Bill Cosby. And now, I find that I cannot. And I gotta tell ya, I never expected that.

Therefore here I am—far from wise, entering the golden years with nothing profound to say. No advice to leave.

I am simply glad that you have chosen to pay me this great honor while I still have most of my hair and my stomach has not yet fully obscured my shoe tops. Because you and I both know when the lust for eating and the fire for life embers down to no more than a flicker, silhouetted against the far horizon of a hazy memory, that ain't the most appropriate time to be inviting nobody to dinner. Therefore my deepest and sincerest "thank you" to the distinguished members of the board for catching me just in time. Yet, magnificent

Sidney with director Richard Brooks on the set of *Blackboard Jungle* (1955), a drama set in an interracial high school and released in the wake of the landmark Supreme Court decision in *Brown v. Board of Education*.

though all this is, I must confess to—how shall I put it—feeling just a bit uneasy.

The hands of many human beings are pressed into the molding of a life, and this life standing before you tonight would not be here were it not for the nurturing it received from many the world has made little note of. I must pause here, if this marvelous evening is not to fall short. If my uneasiness is to be dissolved. I must share tonight with them, and them with you. The first and foremost of them—her name is Evelyn. Evelyn Outten Poitier, my mother. She, most of all, is the reason I am here tonight and for her (most of all), I am proud to be here tonight. Her husband, Reginald James Poitier, my dad. A good, solid, loving fellow, who stood tall through times that would rattle a fortress. My sister, Verdon Poitier Williams, fearless and curious. A freer spirit I have yet to meet. To know her was to know how to be at home in every corner of the world. My friends Harry Johnson, Yorick Rolle, and Joe Palashie, who lived fast and died young and left me with childhood memories that have helped to light my way. An elderly Jewish waiter who took the time to help a young Black dishwasher learn how to read. Night after night, week after week, he persevered—with patience. I cannot tell you his name. I never knew it. But I read pretty good now. I share this evening with him. And all the unknown loving hands that have pushed me gently along the way.

And then there are those who have left a very special mark on the world and me—and this old world, and me, are the better for it. Inspiration is an energizer. I know—having had to travel such a long distance to get here. Inspiration kept my tank full over long, lonely years. And no better time, than now, to thank some of those whose lives supplied me with all I needed. Thank you, Alice Childress, Canada Lee, Paul Robeson, Martin Luther King Jr., Thurgood Marshall, Jackie Robinson, Ruby Dee, Lorraine Hansberry. And last, but not least, that old decrepit folk singer, What's-His-Name Belafonte.

To my love, my wife, my life force, my inspiration, my Joanna—the most loving, caring person I have ever known. All my love always for twenty-four years of happiness. To my six children—three of whom have jobs, which ain't no bad percentage in these uncertain times—to them, my love and thanks, too. To my grandchildren, fifteen and seventeen, whom I certainly expect to be working full time any day now. To each and every one of you, I will remain forever indebted. And I shall gather each fantastic moment in this once-in-a-lifetime evening and store them close to a grateful heart, exactly where priceless memories are likely to be kept.

My thanks to George Stevens Jr., a man of integrity with whom I enjoy a friendship of substance; to Ms. Jean Firstenberg, the talented and charming director of the

Sidney and costar Rod Steiger on the set of *In the Heat of the Night* (1967), winner of the Best Picture Oscar, in which Sidney portrays police detective Virgil Tibbs, one of his most iconic roles.

American Film Institute; and the members of the Academy.

My thanks also go to that community of filmmakers who made room for me to be—and room for me to grow. Much of this evening is due to you, Stanley Kramer, may God bless your maverick soul. And you, Walter Mirisch, and you, Joe Mankiewicz, and you, Richard Brooks, and the multitude of others who have eased my way. Thank you all for having helped mine to be one hell of a journey.

To the young African American filmmakers who have arrived on the playing field, I am filled with pride that you are here. I am sure you have, like me, discovered it was never impossible; it was just harder. It is gratifying to see, and may the world take note, that you didn't let harder stop you. Welcome, young-bloods! Those of us who go before you glance back with satisfaction and leave you with a simple trust. Be true to yourselves and be useful to the journey.

Finally to Sony-Columbia, for treating me like family these past twenty-five years and for two days ago paying great honor to my father's name.

Now, I'd better take Harry home. All this excitement is too risky for a man of his age. It was, for me, an evening that I shall always remember. You have given me reasons to reach farther than I've ever reached in my life. This certainly puts new goals far outside the points of my fingers. Thank you.

NAACP IMAGE AWARDS

Hall of Fame Award
February 23, 2001
Universal Amphitheatre, Los Angeles, California

This was hardly Sidney's first interaction with the NAACP, having been on the front lines of the struggle for civil rights in the 1960s. He had even been given a previous award from the organization when, in November 1993, he and Harry Belafonte were together presented with the Thurgood Marshall Lifetime Achievement Award.

Started in 1983, the Image Awards Hall of Fame is an honor reserved for those of the highest artistic achievement whose work has stood the test of time. For Sidney's tribute, Morgan Freeman introduced fellow actors Sean Patrick Thomas, Andre Braugher, and Michael Clarke Duncan—each of whom read a passage directly from one of Sidney's autobiographies. His daughters then presented a video package of his screen roles, and musical performances were given by James Ingram, Chaka Khan, Gerald Levert, Natalie Cole, and Lou Rawls. The thirty-second annual NAACP Image Awards, honoring the work of African Americans in film, television, music, and literature—and today, podcasting and social media—were televised on Fox.

Nearly sixty years ago, when I was in my teens, each time I thought of myself as being no less than any man and that my dreams were as valid as I was prepared to make them, this organization was there speaking with encouragement on my behalf. That same encouragement resounded through the years and was always on hand to inspire us all to stand firm, hold our ground, and refuse to be moved whenever the question of survival was at stake.

That encouragement sent the great Thurgood Marshall into dangerous territory on legal missions of mercy on behalf of our lives. He was sent by this organization to face off against the multitude of unjust laws that surrounded us. And here tonight, all the admirable conditions that make these awards possible at this time in American history is due to an appreciable degree to the efforts of this organization and others like it. Therefore, I share this award with the past, present, and future members of the NAACP, the very organization that has done so much to make this evening possible.

I stand on this stage tonight in the presence of my fellow actors, who stand today partially because of the NAACP, among the finest actors in the world. These were the kind of

... each time I thought of myself as being no less than any man and that my dreams were as valid as I was prepared to make them, this organization was there speaking with encouragement on my behalf.

actors who in fact were not allowed to represent us when I was a boy. I am so happy to be in their presence in this generation of mine, representing your boys and your girls.

I shall remember this evening forever, and I thank everyone concerned with this

Morgan Freeman took part in the NAACP Image Awards tribute to Sidney.

most prestigious honor, and I promise you I shall spend the rest of my life exemplifying that I have been worthy of it.

ACADEMY HONORARY AWARD

March 24, 2002
Kodak Theatre, Los Angeles, California

When Sidney won the Academy Award for Best Actor for *Lilies of the Field* on April 13, 1964, his speech was quite short: "Because it is a long journey to this moment, I am naturally indebted to countless numbers of people, principally among whom are Ralph Nelson, James Poe, William Barrett, Martin Baum, and of course the members of the Academy. For all of them, all I can say is a very special thank-you." He ended his time at the podium grinning from ear to ear, visibly emotional about the magnitude of the honor. Perhaps he had planned to say more, and he finally got the chance nearly four decades later when the Academy's board of governors voted to present him with an Honorary Award.

At the seventy-fourth Academy Awards ceremony in 2002, Denzel Washington introduced a video montage of Sidney's performances. He was then joined by producer Walter Mirisch, producer of *In the Heat of the Night* (1967), to present the Oscar to Sidney "in recognition of his remarkable accomplishments as an artist and as a human being."

An hour later, Washington would give his own acceptance speech for Best Actor, for *Training Day* (2001). He praised the groundbreaking actor again, saying, "I'll always be chasing you, Sidney. I'll always be following in your footsteps. There's nothing I would rather do, sir. Nothing I would rather do. God bless you." In a historic night, Halle Berry also became the first woman of color to win Best Actress for her performance in *Monster's Ball* (2001).

I arrived in Hollywood at the age of twenty-two in a time different than today's, a time in which the odds against my standing here tonight fifty-three years later would not have fallen in my favor. Back then, no route had been established for where I was hoping to go, no pathway left in evidence for me to trace, no custom for me to follow.

Yet, here I am this evening at the end of a journey that in 1949 would have been con-

sidered almost impossible and in fact might never have been set in motion were there not an untold number of courageous, unselfish choices made by a handful of visionary American filmmakers, directors, writers, and producers, each with a strong sense of citizenship responsibility to the times in which they lived, each unafraid to permit their art to reflect their views and values, ethical and moral, and moreover, acknowledge them as their own. They knew the odds that stood against them, and their efforts were overwhelming and likely could have proven too high to overcome. Still those filmmakers persevered, speaking through their art to the best in all of us. And I've benefited from their effort. The industry benefited from their effort. America benefited from their effort. And in ways large and small the world has also benefited from their effort.

Therefore, with respect, I share this great honor with the late Joe Mankiewicz; the late Richard Brooks; the late Ralph Nelson; the late Darryl Zanuck; the late Stanley Kramer; the Mirisch brothers, especially Walter, whose friendship lies at the very heart of this moment; Guy Green; Norman Jewison; and all others who have had a hand in altering the odds for me and for others. Without

An Academy member since 1965, Sidney was presented with an honorary Oscar in 2002 for his decades of extraordinary work in the American film industry.

them, this most memorable moment would not have come to pass and the many excellent young actors who have followed in admirable fashion might not have come as they have to enrich the tradition of American filmmaking as they have. I accept this award in memory of all the African American actors and actresses who went before me in the difficult years, on whose shoulders I was privileged to stand to see where I might go.

My love and my thanks to my wonderful, wonderful wife; my children; my grandchildren; my agent and friend, Martin Baum. And

Sidney at the 2002 Academy Awards with Joanna and daughter Sydney. The ceremony, in which Denzel Washington and Halle Berry also won lead acting awards, was "pregnant with all kinds of things," said Sidney. "It represented progress. It meant the embracing of a kind of democracy that had been very long in maturing. It was an example of the persistence and effort and determination of young people of color. It was a spectacular evening."

finally, to those audience members around the world who have placed their trust in my judgment as an actor and filmmaker, I thank each of you for your support through the years. Thank you.

MARIAN ANDERSON AWARD

November 14, 2006
Philadelphia, Pennsylvania

Sidney knew and admired the legendary African American contralto Marian Anderson, and in 2006 he was selected to receive an award named for her. The honor was originally established by Anderson in 1943 to benefit aspiring singers and today is given more broadly to an artist "whose leadership on behalf of a humanitarian cause or issue benefits society." He was thus among the company of other important musicians and actors such as Quincy Jones, Gregory Peck, Elizabeth Taylor, Ruby Dee and Ossie Davis, Danny Glover, Oprah Winfrey, and his good friend Harry Belafonte.

At the award gala in November, which functioned as a fundraising benefit for philanthropic programs for young classical artists and high school vocalists, host Phylicia Rashad introduced performances by the Philadelphia Orchestra, actress and soprano Audra McDonald, trumpeter Chris Botti, and gospel singer Yolanda Adams, followed by a keynote address by James Earl Jones. Accepting the award, Sidney spoke about the "oneness of the human family," the importance of curiosity, and the legacy of Anderson.

Ladies and gentlemen, I am delighted to be here. My thanks and deepest appreciation to those whose hearts and minds have made this extraordinary evening possible. The hearts and minds of men and women whose daily existence enriches, complements, and reinforces the dignity of human life, in a process that is ever ongoing.

Such are the hearts and minds that have so graciously invited me to come and be received as this evening's honoree.

If I have indeed managed to reflect, in some small measure, at least a few of the values and principles that are the very foundation on which this respected and celebrated Marian Anderson Award so proudly sits, then, ladies and gentlemen, I accept this award with the full knowledge that it will require my very best effort to balance with grace this most distinguished honor you have placed upon my unworthy head. To wear it well, my reach must constantly exceed my grasp.

With such a task ahead, let me begin by taking first things first. I, like all honorees who have preceded me, will try my very best to live up to the level of integrity where expectations are transformed into good deeds well done.

For those of you who might not know me and are here tonight on the strength of your admiration and respect for the lady whose name is indelibly imprinted on this evening, or merely because you find yourself with a mind full of questions or a pocket full of speculations as to who this Sidney Poitier guy actually is...

Philadelphia Mayor John F. Street presents Sidney with the Marian Anderson Award.

Well, to start with, I am taller than I was sixty-four years ago, when as a fifteen-year-old boy I started on a long, complicated journey through life, a boy who has come from a faraway place: along highways, byways, dark alleys, and dusty roads; through muck and mire; across desolate, lonesome valleys; and over the peaks of unmovable mountains... That boy, whose survival mystified logic and reason—and himself—at every turn, even to this moment... That boy is, in every respect, the selfsame Sidney Poitier guy who landed here tonight by the grace of powers far beyond his understanding.

With that said, let us move closer to deeper truths: about you, about me, and about the oneness of the human family. The truths that were exemplified by the life of Marian Anderson. Truths broader than my limited language skills can convey, deeper than the wisest of men can fathom, but luckily truths that speak eloquently for themselves on evenings like this. Evenings that are set aside in order that respect is paid and obligations reaffirmed to those truths already enshrined in our hearts and left there in safekeeping as part of the invaluable legacy we each have inherited from the lives of ancestors long gone. Ordinary men, ordinary women—of courage, of character, of perseverance, and of honor—whose blood still runs in the veins of each person gathered here this evening.

As the future unfolds, I will try as best I can as a new honoree to reinforce those truths with some of yours, some of mine, and some from the oneness of the human family. I will try to never forget that as human beings we are inextricably intertwined in more ways than we can possibly imagine, which makes almost anything possible, which in turn leaves the human family with more challenges than we can possibly keep track of.

But nature, in her wisdom, loaded us down with a priceless gift: curiosity, which compels us, drives us to go sticking our noses into her business, looking for answers, trying to figure out how things work. Trying to understand the mysteries of the universe and how it came to be as it is. But it was a good thing, that gift called curiosity. Even though we complain and grumble, we begrudgingly accept that we and nature are necessary players on a larger stage.

Most of all, I will try to remember, having once read it somewhere, that when the peace is fragile and turmoil threatens the world, the future seeks refuge in strong hearts and steady hands. How strong the hearts, how steady the hands, will determine how well we continue to handle the challenges nature will surely continue to send our way.

Remember too that our ancestors are ever near, to keep us mindful as to whether we are standing on the plus or minus side of the common ground. As a new honoree I expect I will be consulting my ancestors slightly more often than usual.

My thanks to you, ladies and gentlemen, and to the legacy of an extraordinary American lady, Marian Anderson. My thanks also to the beautiful Phylicia Rashad, the incomparable James Earl Jones, the company of talented musicians and performing artists. Thank you all.

THE LINCOLN MEDAL

February 11, 2009
Ford's Theatre, Washington, DC

The Lincoln Medal is an award given by Ford's Theatre Society to a public figure who, "through his or her body of work, accomplishments or personal attributes, exemplifies the lasting legacy and mettle of character embodied by the most beloved president in our nation's history, President Abraham Lincoln." In 2009, Sidney was a recipient along with Aretha Franklin and George Lucas. He was once again introduced by actor James Earl Jones.

He speaks of unprecedented challenges for the country, no doubt referring to the financial crisis of 2008, commonly referred to as the "Great Recession." The ceremony occurred in the first few weeks of the presidency of Barack Obama, whom Sidney—a staunch Democrat—had met months earlier at a campaign event and whose presence graced Ford's Theatre that night. In his speech, he speaks very proudly of what he sees as the shared characteristics of Obama and Lincoln. Inarguably, Sidney's artistic legacy was one of the many stepping stones that led to the election of the nation's first African American president.

Sidney would go on to be awarded the Presidential Medal of Freedom by President Obama in August 2009.

Mr. President, Mrs. Obama, distinguished guests, ladies and gentlemen, I am extremely honored to receive this award from Ford's Theatre and am deeply humbled to accept an award that associates my name and work with one of the greatest figures in American history: President Abraham Lincoln. The work that President Lincoln began with the Emancipation Proclamation and the Thirteenth Amendment endured beyond his tragic assassination in this theater. Yet, as we gather here this evening, his life, his work, his values are still very, very much alive—alive in our homes, on our streets, in our towns, in our cities, in every one of these United States.

And now, finally, we have lived to see the election of an African American to the highest office in the land. That speaks volumes,

not only of Abraham Lincoln, but also of the multitude of this nation's citizens who have found room in their hearts to receive the values of both President Lincoln and President Barack Obama. Everyone sitting in this room knows this is not the end of the struggle, the struggle that Abraham Lincoln was born to address. The great work of President Lincoln continues and will continue for generations to come.

As in Lincoln's time, our country faces challenges that seem insurmountable, challenges that tear at the very fibers that bind us together. It is, perhaps, for this reason that this nation looks once again to President Abraham Lincoln for inspiration and hope.

And then came a young man of simple origins, who sits in our midst this evening, to remind us that intelligence, eloquence, compassion, determination, courage, tenac-

Sidney received the Lincoln Medal alongside filmmaker George Lucas, seen here with his wife Mellody Hobson, First Lady Michelle Obama, and the president.

ity, and a passionate belief in the ideals upon which this country was founded can guide us through the most difficult of times. It is these qualities that made President Lincoln great, and it is these qualities that inspired this young man of simple origins—and many other Americans—to bring to their life's work inspiration, passion, and hope.

That Ford's Theatre has chosen to recognize such as my modest accomplishments have been is profoundly moving to me, and I thank all concerned with the design of this memorable evening. I can promise each of you that this evening will warm my heart in the winters to come. Thank you—thank you very much for your kind attention and this most remarkable honor.

PERSEVERANCE…

DETERMINATION…

COMMITMENT…

ARE HUMAN QUALITIES — PASSED

ALONG — THROUGH THE BLOOD OF

ANCESTORS LONG GONE.

ALL OF WHICH, AND MORE,

WERE — REQUIRED IN THE MIX,

IN ORDER — THAT THOSE HONORED

HERE THIS EVENING,

OVERBURDENED AS THEIR LONG

JOURNEY HAS BEEN, THEY ARE

HERE. EACH WITH HARD-EARNED

CREDENTIALS ACKNOWLEDGED.
AND RESPECTED

AMONG THEM — IS AN OLD SOLDIER

— WHO STOOD HIS GROUND —

DESIGNED HIS OWN JOURNEY: AND

PAINTED — HIS OWN LANDSCAPE.

A SOLDIER I ADMIRE GREATLY.

HE TRAVELED — LONELY

ROADWAYS AND LEFT BEHIND —

FOOTPRINTS OF HIS CULTURE.

IN ADDITION,

NATURE HAS GIFTED HIM —

WITH A SON — WHO HAS PROVEN

PAUL ROBESON SPEECH

for

6/1/98 Robey Theater Tribute

Robeson. You have read about Paul Robeson. You have seen

paintings, statues, possibly plaques and awards granted

the man's education, his talents, his professional life.

nsional view, of this remarkable person is through the

years.

it. When I was 25 he was 53. Between us handshakes

many. He visited my home, played with my then two

man, and to, ultimately, demolish the man, himself. An effort that la

for more than forty years.

as there such a need on the part of such a nation to break such a n

ation see him as a threat instead of as a gift? The true answer to t

ospectively, is astounding. Of all the educated professionals in all of

d disciplines of science, technology, the legal profession and the nume

ss establishments necessary to develop and keep the american indus

ble and strong, there was no room for this accomplished, professional m

impeccable credentials, an exceptional intellect and the determinatic

to his country, his culture and his people. The nation couldn't find r

to accommodate this extraordinary human being - One of it's finest s

because he also brought with him the color of his skin? Looking back

THE LEGACY OF BLACK HOLLYWOOD

It did not start with me. Nor did I come
out of nowhere. I followed.

Sidney's career was—and remains—a major milestone in the history of African American cinema. As film historian Donald Bogle has noted, "In the 1960s, Sidney Poitier carried Black movie history on his shoulders."

He frequently portrayed resolute men characterized by their dignity. He did this most famously in *Guess Who's Coming to Dinner*, a film that strategically isolated his skin color—rather than his language, career, culture, family values, education, or manners—as the sticking point for the film's white characters, thereby pointing out the absurdity of pure racism. Such a movie role could have easily just been a powerless cipher for liberal white filmmakers, but Poitier's dynamism, steely resolve, and clear self-esteem raised these types of performances to the level of greatness.

Perhaps it was inevitable that after his blockbuster period in the late 1960s—though he continued to work steadily for decades—his career would be the yardstick by which many Black filmmakers and actors who came after him would be judged. And as he continued to act and even direct his own movies, he became a sort of elder statesman of Black American cinema, befriending and nurturing new artists while paying tribute to the legacy that he and others helped establish.

"I was possible only because of those who went before me," he told an audience at a Black Filmmakers Hall of Fame ceremony. A remarkable group of Black actors and actresses whose effort, under unimaginable restrictions, hammered out a path that eased my way." At several events, including honors given to him and tributes given by him to other major Black artists, Sidney continued to pay tribute to those who paved the way for him and those he worked with—while passing the torch to a new generation of talent.

BLACK MOVIE AWARDS

Distinguished Career Achievement Award
October 9, 2005
Wiltern Theatre, Los Angeles, California

"The Black Movie Awards: A Celebration of Black Cinema—Past, Present & Future" was hosted by Cedric the Entertainer and aired on TNT on October 19, 2005. The ceremony honored Black filmmaking achievements for the year, and a major highlight was a career tribute to Sidney.

Here, he pays homage to friends and colleagues with whom he worked at the beginning of his career in New York, including Julian Mayfield (discreetly referred to as a "successful novelist") and William Greaves (a "highly honored documentary filmmaker").

Fifty-eight years ago in New York City, I was one in a group of about twelve or so young African American actors of roughly the same age who were in constant and fierce competition for any and all of the few parts that came up. The three or four guys most likely to have been cast were some good-looking dudes, and damn good actors on top of that.

In the summer of 1949, word spread that 20th Century Fox was looking for a young African American actor to play a doctor who worked in a county hospital for a movie called *No Way Out*. We all showed up at the 20th Century Fox casting office on West 57th Street in New York. The good-looking dudes came in looking exactly like young doctors should look. We all knew from past experiences that the good-looking guys had the edge. The rest of us came in, hoping the part was that of an ordinary-looking, run-of-the-mill kind of doctor with a great bedside manner, instead of just plain old good looks—a quality for which the others of us definitely fell short.

As for me? By my own objective assessment, my chances were not good—by any stretch of the imagination. Still, I got the part. What did that tell me? What did I learn? I learned that my getting that job was part of an unfathomable process that began unfolding—and continued unfolding—over the following fifty-eight years to this moment, as I am standing here, saying thank you for this award.

It appears now that God, nature, destiny, serendipity, chance, luck, karma, and twists of fate hold stronger hands in our lives than we do. That is not a judgment. It is an observation that leads me to take a closer look at the hand I hold in my own life, which includes the obligation to think for myself. If one can play their hand well, then the rest of existence is in the hands of forces infinitely more powerful. That is my view, and I, for one, respect-

If one can play their hand well, then the rest of existence is in the hands of forces infinitely more powerful.

fully leave to them how they choose to play their hand in what is left of this life of mine.

The rest of our original dozen or so went wherever their lives have taken them. One became a successful novelist and a lecturer at Howard University. Another became a world-renowned and highly honored documentary filmmaker. Many others found success along different pathways. A few died young. I wish them well, wherever they are at this moment. Each of their names is symbolically written on this award. I thank you in their names. As for myself, this award means as much to me as any award I have ever received.

Sidney's character engages in an interracial romance in *A Patch of Blue* (1965), a black-and-white film about the colorblindness of love.

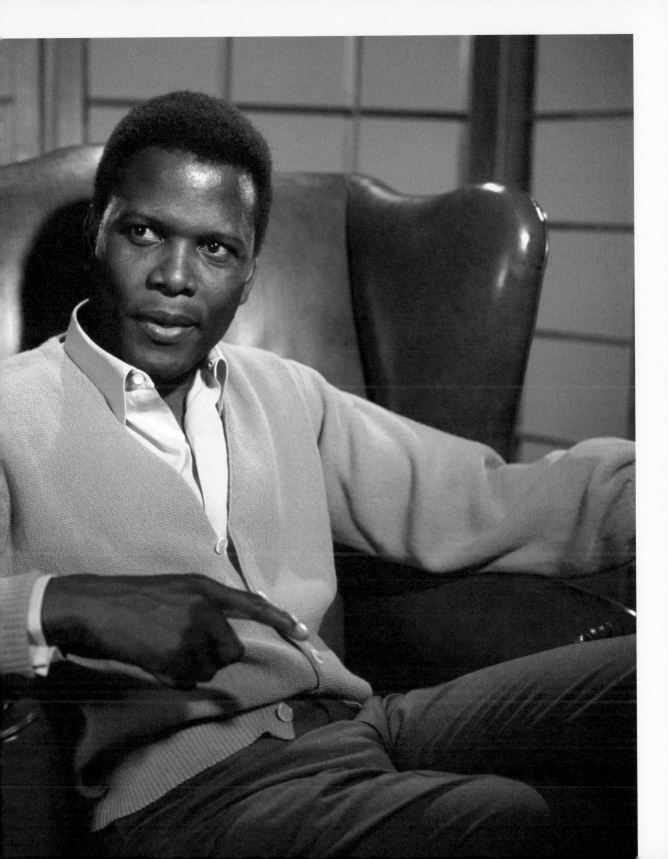

BERRY GORDY

The Brotherhood Crusade's Black Achievement Award
December 8, 1988
Beverly Hilton Hotel, Beverly Hills, California

Record producer and songwriter Berry Gordy, a good friend of Sidney's, was honored by the Brotherhood Crusade with its twentieth annual Black Achievement Award in 1988, recognizing "achievement by a role model for youth." Sidney spoke in tribute to Gordy at the philanthropic group's fundraising dinner in Beverly Hills.

When a man is excellent company for his friends and wonderful company for himself, he bears watching. When balance and peace centers him in an unsteady world, we should draw closer and listen to his life. It is for a reason that he walks with purpose and speaks with candor.

Get close enough and the generosity of spirit that lights his way will also warm your heart. Over the past years it has often come to my mind that my friend Berry Gordy is such a man. When a remarkable honor is paid a friend, I am gratified. But not nearly so much as now, when the friend is here with us in the healthy bloom of his middle years, to receive it, taste of it, and walk away—on to other challenges—leaving behind this unique reminder of victories won, risks taken, choices made.

In our business, creative instinct walks a long, lonely line daily. On the occasion it falters, we taste of defeat. When it stays steadfast and true, it brings us to nights like these, when tributes are in order and a collective "thank you" is loudly proclaimed.

Berry Gordy Jr., my friend, I am sure you will go on to greater things yet, in the process of which you will be able to hire all the actors who have never worked for you—a category in which I have found myself for many years. I don't know how many more of your honors you expect me to live through before you take notice of my situation.

Congratulations, Berry. The choice made by the Brotherhood Crusade was first-rate and long overdue.

Upon Sidney's passing in 2022, Motown Records founder Berry Gordy Jr. spoke eloquently of his long-time friend. "He was a man of grace, integrity, and someone I long admired. He is in a class by himself."

HARRY BELAFONTE

Kennedy Center Honors
December 2, 1989
Washington, DC

Sidney paid tribute to his dear friend Harry Belafonte—a man whose name frequently appears in Sidney's speeches—joined in a surprise visit by Archbishop Desmond Tutu. Sidney himself would receive a Kennedy Center Honor in 1995.

We first met as students in a cramped storage area directly underneath the stage of a community theater group called the American Negro Theatre. There in the semidarkness, we sized each other up while rummaging for old pieces of prop and stage dressings for a student production we were both hoping to get into. In those moments, territorial boundaries were psychologically drawn, competitive positions were taken, the seeds of mutual respect were planted.

Now, forty-three years later, after all the words have been spoken, after most of our dreams have been turned into memories, I am glad to have made that journey with such a man, such an artist, such an activist, such a father, such a friend.

I am older than he by eight days. He is older than I by wisdom and tenacity. We have learned together, suffered together, laughed together, struggled together, traveled Africa together, drawn by our common roots. I believe your regrets are few—and a few regrets is as good a score as most of us gathered here will manage.

And how you have enriched our country. There has always been folk music in America, but it was you who gave it new shading and meaning, and the spirit of other lands. You rolled up your sleeves and unbuttoned your shirt—down to here [points to his own

Sidney at the March on Washington on August 28, 1963, with Belafonte, who spoke at the landmark event.

navel]—and, fast as Matilda could run Venezuela, you had us all singing with an accent. Harry Belafonte is a man who has always rallied to good causes. He has always raised his voice against the dark. For that, we owe him so much.

Harry B., my old young friend, I am so proud to see you honored by your country, which speaks volumes for you and volumes for your beloved country.

SAMMY DAVIS JR.

NAACP Image Awards
Hall of Fame Award
December 9, 1989
Wiltern Theatre, Los Angeles, California

The Hollywood branch of the NAACP created the Image Awards in 1967 to honor the achievements of Black artists in film and television, and later expanding to the fields of music and literature. Sammy Davis Jr. was one of the leaders of the branch and an original organizer of the Image Awards. His induction into the Hall of Fame at the twenty-second ceremony in 1989 was introduced by Sidney.

Tonight, we look upon the giant statue of a remarkable man who, for sixty long years, has moved among us, bringing his priceless gift to warm our hearts, and we continue to behold him with wonder. This small-framed man upon whose shoulders generations of entertainers have stood is truly the quintessential performer of the twentieth century. He is a pearl perfected in the tumultuous days when America was obliged to take a hard look at herself; he is a diamond forged deep in the earth of his ancestors' culture, a gem in which, when held up to the sun, one can see every color and hue in the spectrum of humanity, compassion, talent, and life. This small-framed man, this phenomenon, started out in vaudeville as a child in a spotlight, and through sixty dazzlingly delightful years, amazed us with a talent one thousand times larger than the frame God chose to house it in.

New light need not be shed on the fact that he is a concerned human being who has given time and money in the fight against poverty and racial intolerance. Nor need we be reminded that before the cultural boycott, he stood by the principle of not performing in apartheid South Africa.

They have asked me here tonight to induct this remarkable man, this small-framed phenomenon, this Sammy Davis Jr. person, into the NAACP Hall of Fame. I personally want him to know it is an honor, and he will always be welcomed in our hearts.

Sammy Davis Jr. and his mother, Elvera Sanchez Davis,
with Sidney at a Friars Club event in April 1966

WHOOPI GOLDBERG

American Cinema Awards—Distinguished
Achievement in Film Award
September 12, 1992
Beverly Hilton Hotel, Beverly Hills, California

Music publicist and manager David Gest launched the American Cinema Awards Foundation in 1983 as a fundraising effort for a memorabilia museum but quickly transitioned its focus to charitable causes. In 1992, Whoopi Goldberg was honored with a Distinguished Achievement in Film award at the ninth annual ceremony, alongside honors for Frank Sinatra and MPAA president Jack Valenti. Robert Wagner was the host and Kirk and Anne Douglas were chairs of the dinner. The proceeds went to the Motion Picture and Television Fund's Harry's Haven Alzheimer's unit.

To most of us, nature has assigned modest tools with which we must try to chisel, inch by inch, a useful and productive path through life. Modest tools in the hands of most of us sometimes barely manage to get the job done—even modestly. Sometimes ourselves and our tools are insufficient to the task. Sometimes, on the other hand, there is Whoopi Goldberg—who wasn't assigned modest tools like the rest of us. Nature had to go and overload the child with a great personality, a ton of talent, a smile that lights up the whole world, and a presence on screens big and small that seduces us instantly. However, nature did temper her generosity by giving Whoopi a short fuse. And like the rest of us, when she gets pissed, she gets pissed. But that you already know. Seriously—here is what you may not know. Not a day passes that she does not say thank you to someone for a thoughtful gesture, a favor done. She says thank you to friends for a show of support over tough times, for lending themselves as cushions when doubt gathers and confidence loses its balance. She says thank you when she escapes misfortune's path by a hair's breadth, by a heartbeat, or by the miracle of chance. She says thank you when prayers are heard and answered and she is left in wonder of the process. We have gathered here tonight

"He showed us how to reach for the stars," wrote Goldberg upon Sidney's passing in 2022.

to say a collective "thank you" to her for having so often touched our hearts and left us with indelible memories. Ladies and gentlemen, it is my pleasure to present this award to the one and only Whoopi Goldberg.

QUINCY JONES

The American Society of Music Arrangers and
Composers Golden Score Awards Dinner
December 2, 1994
Universal Hilton, Los Angeles, California

Having originally met him at the Birdland Jazz Club in New York City, Sidney crossed professional paths with music producer, composer, arranger, and songwriter Quincy Jones many times, including on the films *In the Heat of the Night, They Call Me Mr. Tibbs!, The Slender Thread,* and *The Lost Man,* for which Jones composed original music. The American Society of Music Arrangers and Composers was founded in 1938, with the first Golden Score Award presented four decades later. In 1994, Jones joined an illustrious group of previous honorees including Elmer Bernstein, Henry Mancini, John Williams, and Jerry Goldsmith.

Billy Eckstine was once heard to say that Quincy Jones is one pretty "bleep bleep." Nearly forty years ago, I bore witness to that fact. I was idly standing about in the middle of the block on the west side of Broadway, gawking across the street at the entrance of the world famous Birdland Jazz Club, when a young man stepped out of the club and headed across the street. I had heard of but had never met Quincy Jones, and didn't know what he looked like. In an instant, I heard the name whispered by a young lady passing by, and I noticed that the heads of every woman in that block had turned towards the center of the street. They were each galvanized by the presence of the young man ambling his way across Broadway. And let me tell you, Eckstine was right. The man was prettier than Muhammad Ali. Dressed in drop-dead Paris fashion, he moved with the ease of someone who had 51 percent ownership of planet Earth. I spoke to him: "Hello, Mr. Jones." "Hi there, how are you doing?" Right then and there, I wanted to grow up to be like Quincy Jones—even though I was already nearly ten years older than he. He was great with the guys and smooth with the ladies.

I grew to appreciate the esteem in which he was held by his peers. They recognized,

early, his creative abilities as a musician and his genius as a composer. I was not as readily perceptive because I possess a notoriously weak knowledge of music, which is based on a genetically inherited inability to carry a tune. I have hoped for forty-six years that Harry Belafonte and Quincy Jones could and would rectify that oversight of nature. Harry has flatly refused, saying that he knows no African American who can't sing. And he is delighted to have me as an example to the contrary. I waited additional years for Quincy to correct the minor flaw. But alas, over time, Quincy agreed with Harry, leaving me to live out my days as an example to the contrary. But never

Sidney and Quincy Jones met in New York City in the 1950s, kicking off a lifelong friendship. "He had such a kind spirit, and I knew it wouldn't be the last time we saw each other," Quincy recalled. They soon began a productive working relationship as well, starting with the 1965 film *The Slender Thread*.

mind—I will close my remarks with these few words I once wrote about Quincy Jones.

When a man is excellent company for his friends and wonderful company for himself, he bears watching. When balance and peace center him in an unsteady world, we should draw closer and listen to his life. It is for a reason that he walks with purpose and speaks with candor.

Sidney and Jones share a touching moment.

Get close enough, and the generosity of spirit that lights his way will also warm your heart. Over the past years it has often come to my mind that my friend Quincy Jones is such a man.

When a remarkable honor is paid a friend, I am gratified. But not nearly so much as now, when the friend is here with us in the healthy bloom of his middle years, to receive it, taste of it, and walk away—on to other challenges—leaving behind this unique reminder of victories won, risks taken, choices made.

In our business, creative instinct walks a long, lonely line daily. On the occasion it falters, we taste of defeat. When it stays steadfast and true, it brings us to nights like these, when tributes are in order and a collective "thank you" is loudly proclaimed.

Seriously though, Quincy, we shall never be able to pay our debt to you in full. We hope this day will always remind you of our appreciation for your having taken us on journeys of sound that soothed our minds and captivated our interest, for surrounding our quiet nights with melodies, rhythms, and tempos that refreshed, delighted, and made spicy many otherwise ordinary evenings.

For tears of joy and sadness, for laughter and laid-back good times, we owe you. For jump-starting the spirit of adventure that lies all too dormant in too many of us, we owe you. For the beautiful places your music transported us to, we owe you. But most of all we owe you for having the mind of a great musician and the hypnotic skills of a truly gifted composer. We, your listeners and your friends, ask only that you keep us in your debt.

PAUL ROBESON

Robey Theatre Company Tribute
June 1, 1998
Actors' Gang Theater, Los Angeles, California

Sidney considered the early twentieth-century singer, actor, and activist Paul Robeson a personal hero and even narrated a 1979 biographical short film—*Paul Robeson: Tribute to an Artist*—which won an Academy Award. In 1998, the Robey Theatre Company, a Los Angeles nonprofit theatre company founded by actors Danny Glover and Ben Guillory, hosted a theatrical tribute for Robeson that raised money for a scholarship fund in the late actor's name administered through Rutgers University. The "anonymous" poem quoted at the conclusion is an altered version of "To Risk" by American writer William Arthur Ward.

You have heard about Paul Robeson. You have read about Paul Robeson. You have seen photographs, motion pictures, paintings, statues, possibly plaques and awards granted to Paul Robeson. You know about the man's education, his talents, his professional life. But the clearest view, the most dimensional view, of this remarkable person is through the prism of the America of his adult years.

I was there for much of it. When I was twenty-five, he was fifty-three. Between us, handshakes were many. Embraces were many. He visited my home, played with my then two youngsters. I attended concerts and rallies where he spoke. And was very often privileged to engage him in conversation of such length and depth as I was capable of, which—let me hasten to add—wasn't much. For being in his presence could tie one's tongue. But I was a good listener, of unbounded admiration. I was present at his concert on that terrifying day in Peekskill, New York, where the road leading into, and out of, the meadow where he performed was lined on both sides by multitudes of haters, with baseball bats and assorted other weapons, intent on doing harm. I was in a car with a fellow actor. The windows were rolled up, the lock buttons were down. By the time we had gotten out of Peekskill, there were no windows left in the car and we were

character, the career, the dignity, the integrity of the man and to ultimately demolish the man himself. An effort that lasted at full intensity for more than forty years.

Why was there such a need on the part of such a nation to break such a man? Why did the nation see him as a threat instead of as a gift? The true answer to these questions, retrospectively, is astounding. Of all the educated professionals in all of the categories and disciplines of science, technology, the legal profession, and the numerous other business establishments necessary to develop and keep the American industrial complex viable and strong, there was no room for this accomplished, professional man—who came with impeccable credentials, an exceptional intellect, and the determination to be of service to his country, his culture, and his people. The nation couldn't find room within itself to accommodate this extraordinary human being—one of its finest sons. Could it be because he also brought with him the color of his skin? Looking back now through the prism of the America of his adult years, one can clearly see the insanity, the vulgarity, the cruelty, and the inhumanity that fueled the national mindset on all issues of color and race.

In the America of Paul Robeson's adult years, and the years of his father and his father's father, exclusion by color habitually won out over inclusion by merit. The national mindset justified its actions by pointing

"Occasionally there comes a guy like Paul Robeson," wrote Sidney in *The Measure of a Man*. "When these people come along, their anger, their rage, their resentment, their frustration—these feelings ultimately mature by their own discipline into a positive energy."

lucky to be alive. That was a very real part of the America of Paul Robeson's adult years, in which a massive array of public, private, and government forces were unleashed with the objective in mind to strip away the image, the at his politics, fully aware that millions of other African Americans who had no politics whatsoever were also denied and excluded by the destructive network of segregation laws that had been called for and set in place by the national mindset. Laws, all too often backed up by the custom of intimidation, intentionally designed to restrict their choices of where they could work, what kind of jobs they could have, what schools they could attend, what churches, what playgrounds their children could enter, where they were allowed to seek entertainment. That is the fact of how it was. The national mindset knew those were the real issues Paul Robeson spoke to, fought for, and spent his life trying to get his fellow Americans to turn their attention to. For African Americans of my generation, and of course for the generations preceding us, we were all blessed and privileged to have had among ourselves men like Paul Robeson, Thurgood Marshall, Ralph Bunche, A. Philip Randolph, Langston Hughes, Canada Lee, John Hope Franklin, William Leo Hansberry, William Hastie, Adam Clayton Powell, Malcolm X, and Martin Luther King, and women like Mary McLeod Bethune, Rosa Parks, Dorothy Height, Marian Edelman, and Fanny Lou Hamer, and thousands more less famous, whose individual deeds were monumentally effective at encouraging us to engage those forces, face-to-face, no matter how mammoth and dangerous we might know them to be.

Their lives taught us there was strength in unity—but they were the famous ones. They were backed by hundreds of thousands whose names we will never know. The degree to which succeeding generations have moved forward—and we have indeed moved forward—is the degree to which those African American men and women and the legion of those whose names we will never know must be thanked and remembered.

The spirit of their message is embodied in this anonymous poem:

To laugh is to risk appearing a fool.

To weep is to risk appearing sentimental.

To reach out for another is to risk involvement.

To expose feelings is to risk rejection.

To place your dreams before the crowd is to risk ridicule.

To love is to risk not being loved in return.

To go forward in the face of overwhelming odds is to risk failure.

But risks must be taken because the greatest hazard in life is to risk nothing.

The person who risks nothing, does nothing, has nothing, is nothing.

He may avoid suffering and sorrow,

But he cannot learn, feel, change, grow or love.

Chained by his certitudes, he is a slave, he has forfeited his freedom.

Only a person who dares to risk is free.

DIAHANN CARROLL

Women in Film Lucy Award
September 12, 1998
The Regent Beverly Wilshire, Beverly Hills, California

Academy Award nominee and pioneering TV actress Diahann Carroll was presented with the Lucy Award, an honor that was given annually to a female actor for a career in television, thanks to her work on series like *Julia*, *Naked City*, and *Dynasty*. Carroll and Sidney worked together years earlier on the turbulent *Porgy and Bess* set and the location shoot for *Paris Blues*, resulting in a years-long romantic relationship. The two remained friends throughout their lives, and Sidney proudly introduced her at the 1998 Women in Film awards ceremony.

When I first met this fabulous person, she was a distraction—let me tell you. It wasn't an everyday occurrence to look upon such striking beauty. That was shortly before we started working on *Porgy and Bess*. My head was like on a swivel stick. To my left was Dorothy Dandridge. On my right was Diahann Carroll. A more articulate example of distraction I've never experienced, let me tell you. In fifty-two years of filmmaking, I never had more trouble learning my lines as I did on that movie.

We made two movies together. We would have made many, many more, but Hollywood wasn't very smart in those days. It had a curious sort of fixated point of view in regard to women and minority guys. And Diahann and I, we were a pretty solid example of both. In the case of this remarkable woman you honor here, today, Hollywood did itself a considerable disservice. But, hey, we're not here to dump on what was—and in some ways still is—a not very smart "little boys' club."

We are here to express our appreciation, our thanks, our gratitude, and pay tribute to this American lady whose quite extraordinary gifts, whose demonstrated integrity, charm, and grace, have enlivened, enlightened, and enhanced the world of American theatre, and American music, and American television, and American fashion. As a person, she has always been a class act, this African American

lady who has captained her own ship using talent and dignity as compasses, determination and perseverance as winds for her sails, who charted her course through life's sometimes treacherous, sometimes indifferent waters. Through particularly stormy patches in her life, character and the stars above

Sidney and Carroll copresent at the 36th NAACP Image Awards in March 2005.

saw her safely from port to port. From the moment I first laid eyes on her, if my memory serves correctly, she was already, even then, a lady in the making.

LAURENCE FISHBURNE

Fortieth Birthday Message
July 30, 2001

Among the next generation of young actors who were inspired by and benefited from Sidney's groundbreaking film work was stage and screen star Laurence Fishburne. In 1996, Fishburne costarred with Stephen Baldwin in *Fled,* a remake of Sidney's landmark film *The Defiant Ones.*

While most men are different in appearance, only a few are different at the core. And fewer still are different in ways that cannot be explained. Chosen by some mysterious process we are not meant to unravel, these precious few will live out their lives in long, lonely journeys straight toward the hearts and minds of their fellow human beings. And there, reveal to us the selves we cannot see. The worlds we never knew existed. Show us how wonder and magic awaken inside us when the energy of new ideas ignites our imagination and pulls at our curiosity. Such journeys were destined to be the stuff from which the life's work of Laurence Fishburne would be fashioned.

"Sidney was my North Star," says Fishburne. "He was a sterling example of how to move through the world, specifically as a Black man, but as a man in general."

DENZEL WASHINGTON

Directors Guild Tribute
December 16, 2002
DGA New York Theater, New York, New York

Denzel Washington had won two Oscars by the time his first directorial effort, *Antwone Fisher*, was released in December 2002. As a fellow African American actor-director, Sidney was the ideal figure to toast Washington's entry into the Directors Guild of America, and he took the opportunity to continue the conversation the two began onstage at the Academy Awards earlier that year.

Denzel, I recall your confiding to me, after you had finished *Antwone Fisher*, that you were hooked on directing. That came as no surprise to me.

I understand the film is wonderful, and I am certain all the reasons you are hooked are evidenced on the screen. But don't quit your day job—not yet. Because we will need your brilliance in both categories going forward. Among the many memorable moments on Academy Awards night past—you said you've been chasing me for forty years. Well, now it's your turn to be chased by another—or two, three, or four—young, gifted, and determined newcomers who, hopefully, through your efforts, will not have to endure another artificial forty-year wait like the one your talents finally struck down earlier this year.

I am confident, knowing you as I do, that you will always be there as an inspiration until that day when you will look back and smile—in the knowledge that the continuance—through you to them—and through them to others—will not be artificially interrupted in the years ahead.

> *The example you are—and have been—is of such an exquisite nature that those chasing you will have to be in damn good shape . . .*

The example you are—and have been—is of such an exquisite nature that those chasing you will have to be in damn good shape—have to come, as you did, with form and substance;

Washington and Sidney at the Carousel of Hope Ball in 2016

come, as you did, with a commitment to excellence; come, as you did, with a determination to hit the ground running or they ain't gonna catch you. So make 'em run, Denzel, make 'em run. For continuance's sake, remind them that they must come as you did—with the very best they've got.

Congratulations, from me and my family to you and yours.

PS: I'm glad I went before you because, were I chasing you, you probably would have run me to death. But I believe you still would have gotten the best I had to give.

And remember, the longer you keep them running, the bigger the pension the Guild will send you when you're too tired to run anymore and have to sit down.

Welcome to the Directors Guild.

MELVIN VAN PEEBLES

Melvin Van Peebles's films from the early 1970s represented a distinct shift from Sidney's more mainstream work. Nevertheless, Sidney introduced the director of the landmark blaxploitation film *Sweet Sweetback's Baadasssss Song* (1971) at the Eye on Black organization's 2011 ceremony honoring African Americans in film, along with his son and fellow director, Mario Van Peebles.

Perseverance . . . determination . . . commitment . . . are human qualities, passed along through the blood of ancestors long gone. So are instincts, intuitions, creative imagination, and toughness of mind. All of which, and more, were required in the mix, in order that those honored here this evening, overburdened as their long journey has been, are here. Each with hard-earned credentials acknowledged.

Among them is an old soldier who stood his ground, designed his own journey, and painted his own landscape. A soldier I admire greatly. He traveled lonely roadways and left behind footprints of his culture. In addition, nature has gifted him with a son who has proven himself to be gifted in the extreme. In fact, he is nearly as good as the old soldier himself.

Ladies and gentlemen, it is my pleasure to present this well-earned, well-deserved honor to the old soldier himself, Mr. Melvin Van Peebles.

COLLEGE OF THE BAHAMAS

6/25/99

DRAFT# 3

HANK YOU PRESIDENT _____ HONORABLE
RIME MINISTER, DISTINGUISHED MEMBERS OF
GOVERNMENT, YOUNG LADIES AND GENTLEMEN OF THE
GRADUATING CLASS, YOUR COMPATRIOTS IN THE
CONTINUING STUDENT BODY, FACULTY MEMBERS,
PARENTS AND FRIENDS, I WELCOME YOU TO THIS LONG
WAITED, VERY GOOD AFTERNOON.
EVENING

YOUR PRESENCE HERE SPEAKS OF QU
KEEN INTEREST, VIBRANT CURIOSI
EXPECTATIONS THAT THREATEN TO KEEP
TOES AND MAKE ME REACH BEYOND
WAITING TO BE INTRODUCED TO YOU. I

YOU ARE, IN FACT, ALL THOSE THIN
CURIOUS AND EXPECTANT - IT MEA
TO STRUGGLE TO MEASURE UP, SO T
HAVE TO MEASURE DOWN. I WOULD H

TALKING TO PEOPLE *THAT* MUCH
I IS FIRST, RISKY! BECAUSE MY IG
HAVE NO PLACE TO HIDE FROM YOUR
MINDS LISTENING FOR HISTOR
PHILOSOPHICAL GEMS, POLITIC
SPIRITUAL RESONANCES - AN
GRAMMAR. FORGET IT! YOU WON'
THOSE. ERRORS OF GRAMMAR ARE
ARE LIKELY TO GET. SECOND, IT FLIES

MANY YEARS AGO, I WAS INVITED, TO AN
EVENING, CENTERED AROUND THE MAGICAL
POWERS, OF EDUCATION. AN EVENING THAT
INSTANTLY BEFUDDLED ME. I HAD, AT THAT
POINT IN LIFE, NO IDEA OF THE FUNDAMENTALS
OF EDUCATION — THE USEFULNESS OF IT, THE
UNKNOWN POWER OF IT — HIDDEN AWAY
OUTSIDE THE REACH OF MY CONSCIOUSNESS.

MY PARENTS WERE TOMATO FARMERS. THEIR
REE GIRLS
I WAS —
EASY

AT 15, I WOUND UP IN NEW YORK AS A
DISHWASHER IN A SMALL RESTAURANT IN
QUEENS LONG ISLAND. I WAS ON MY OWN —
MY CHOIC

JT AND

I SURVIVE
TO LEARN
APPROAC
TO DO BE
DIVINE HU
OUT OF SI
AND MAD
WAS THE
WHEN I W

I WAS SIX

NO PLACE TO STAY. IT WAS IN THE DEAD OF
WINTER AND IN AN EFFORT TO STAY WARM, I
FOUND MYSELF SLEEPING ON THE BENCHES IN
THE WAITING ROOM OF THE PENN STATION
RAILWAY TERMINAL.

I WAS ARRESTED, EVENTUALLY, AND TAKEN
INTO CUSTODY BY TWO COPS WHO HELD ME
UNTIL FINGERPRINT RECORDS TURNED UP
NOTHING.

AS I STEPPED OUT OF THE DOOR OF THAT POLIC

STANDING ON THE SHOULDERS OF GIANTS

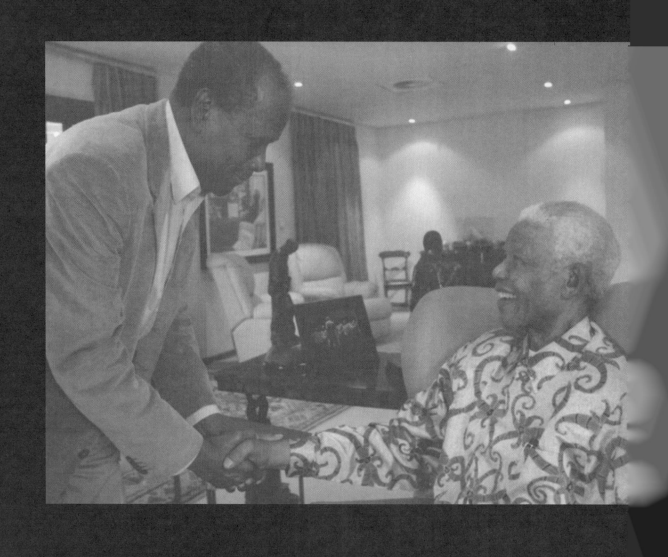

Long before you were born,
there were men and women looking out for you.

Many of Sidney's speeches display an awareness that his unique success is part of a larger arc of history—an epic story of new roads paved, glass ceilings shattered, and doors opened by those who went before him. He saw himself as the recipient of the goodwill and good wishes of his parents and grandparents, the beneficiary of the dedication and ingenuity of civil rights activists, and the fortunate colleague of filmmakers who were trying to make a difference. Therefore, it was incumbent upon him to give as much as he could to those who came after him—both in terms of wisdom and guidance and in the form of vigorous support for education. His longtime support of the Fulfillment Fund and his words at the Jackie Robinson Foundation event are emblematic of this deeply felt mission.

At the same time, he speaks of the importance of struggle—to improve oneself, to make art, to simply get through life in this world—and how we must pick up the mantle that our forebears leave behind and continue their crusade for a better future. These were not abstract concepts for Sidney, whose life and career happened to occur in one of the most dynamic periods of social progress in history, and he often calls upon his own story to give color to his arguments.

OPPOSITE: Sidney with South African President Nelson Mandela, whom he portrayed in the 1997 television film *Mandela and de Klerk*.

THURGOOD MARSHALL
TRIBUTE

After a career as a civil rights lawyer, during which he notably served as chief counsel for the plaintiffs in the landmark 1954 suit *Brown v. Board of Education*, Thurgood Marshall was appointed and confirmed as the first African American justice of the United States Supreme Court in 1967, where he sat until his retirement in 1991. In February 1992, Sidney spoke at a tribute to Justice Marshall hosted by the Jackie Robinson Foundation, which provides scholarships and career counseling to students of color. Sidney had joined Robinson, Harry Belafonte, Martin Luther King Jr., and others in 1959 to launch the African American Students Foundation, and he served on JRF's board of directors from 1979 to 1996.

The struggle for equal justice for all Americans has been fought in many places—from ballparks to lunch counters, from classrooms to courtrooms.

Here at the highest court in the land, a young lawyer named Thurgood Marshall led the fight to make the words "equal justice under law" more than a motto carved in stone.

Thurgood Marshall was born in Baltimore in 1908. His mother was a teacher in a segregated elementary school, his father a steward at an all-white yacht club. They instilled in Thurgood a love of family, and the courage and tenacity to fight for his beliefs.

After graduation from Lincoln University in Pennsylvania, Marshall was denied admission to law school at the University of Maryland because of his color. He enrolled at Howard University, where the great legal scholar Charles Hamilton Houston was vice dean of the law school.

After graduating from Howard with high honors, Marshall opened his own practice in a small office in Baltimore. He joined forces with Houston, then special counsel for the NAACP. They succeeded in getting Donald Murray admitted to law school at the University of Maryland . . . the same school that refused to admit Marshall five years earlier. When Hous-

Sidney portrayed Marshall in the Emmy-winning 1991 television miniseries *Separate but Equal.*

ton stepped down in 1938, Marshall took over as special counsel for the NAACP.

In the 1940s and '50s, as Jackie Robinson was breaking the color barrier in Major League Baseball, Thurgood Marshall was fighting for justice in the courts.

After years of chipping away at inequality case by case, Marshall made a highly contro-

versial move. He challenged the legality of the Supreme Court's 1896 "separate but equal" decision, declaring that separate educational facilities for whites and Blacks "are inherently unequal." But, despite the court's unanimous decision in *Brown v. Board of Education*, Marshall took little time to relax. He warned his colleagues that the work had just begun. He was right. Some states and school systems stalled desegregation, so Marshall made several trips back to the Supreme Court. In 1955, the court ruled that desegregation must be carried out "with all deliberate speed."

The court's "all deliberate speed" clause, was of course, open to interpretation. But for some, even this vague timetable was too much, too soon. Over the next few years, Marshall logged thousands of miles, continuing the battle against segregation.

In 1961, President Kennedy acknowledged Marshall's outstanding legal expertise and bold leadership by appointing him to the Second Circuit Court of Appeals. Four years later, President Johnson named him the first African American solicitor general of the United States.

Thurgood Marshall's career statistics—like Jackie Robinson's—are impressive. But for both of these men, victory was much more than the number of games or cases won.

As a lawyer, federal judge, solicitor general, and Supreme Court justice, Thurgood Marshall helped open doors that had been closed to many Americans. For Justice Marshall, words printed in law books or etched in stone are not the most important elements of democracy.

Thanks to the continuing work of organizations like the NAACP and the NAACP Legal Defense and Educational Fund, we are closer to the ideal of true democracy. Reaching toward Justice Marshall's goal of equality for all Americans, and Jackie Robinson's dream of educational opportunities for everyone, Jackie Robinson scholars and alumni are active participants in the continuing process of positive social change.

Instilled with the spirit of pioneers like Thurgood Marshall and Jackie Robinson, today's young leaders are making their own statements, blazing their own trails, dreaming their own dreams. But they have not forgotten the broad shoulders they stand on. Someday, tomorrow's pioneers will stand on their shoulders.

The Jackie Robinson Foundation takes great pride in paying special tribute to Mr. Thurgood Marshall. From his days as a young lawyer for the NAACP to his retirement from the Supreme Court last year, he helped this nation come closer to realizing the dream of "liberty and justice for all." Asked how he would like to be remembered, Marshall answered that he hoped people would say "he did the best he could with what he had."

We will remember Thurgood Marshall for his integrity, his scholarship, and his activism.

Tonight, we thank him for his untiring dedication and his lasting contributions to America. Most especially, we thank him on behalf of the young people of today . . . and the generations still to come.

CARL FOREMAN
AWARDS LUNCHEON

Carl Foreman was a prolific screenwriter of celebrated films such as *High Noon* (1952), *The Bridge on the River Kwai* (1957), and *The Guns of Navarone* (1961) who was notably exiled from the American film industry as a victim of the Hollywood blacklist. He worked in England for many years and continued to write major scripts but didn't return to the US until the 1970s. The award named in his honor was launched in 1983 in association with the British Academy of Film and Television Arts (BAFTA) to provide scholarship funds to aspiring British students to study filmmaking in America. Sidney spoke at the awards luncheon in May 1993 and presented that year's recipients, Susan Patricia Everett and Belinda Bauer.

Though the two men never worked directly together, Sidney speaks eloquently here about Foreman's character through personal and professional tribulation, citing other people of similar integrity who had made an impact in his own journey through life.

It was in 1967 that I first met the Carl Foreman in whose name we gather here today. And it is with much love and affection that I stand here before you as this twenty-sixth year of our friendship folds into history. Please allow me this moment to share with you what I knew best and what I remember most about Carl Foreman—what was and is the character of the man. His friendship taught me what character was, and his life led me to understand how character is forged in the human personality. It wasn't long after we first met that I came to realize we had met before 1967.

Carl Foreman was a teacher in the Bahamas in the year 1938, who taught me how to read and write. How to look at the horizon where the sea and the sky met and wonder what kind of world could be beyond. Carl Foreman was a Jewish waiter in a restaurant in New York City where I washed dishes. At seventeen years of age there, late evenings after work was done, we would sit and talk. He introduced me to values like integrity, honesty, and fairness, and suggested they become traveling companions on my journey through life. Carl Foreman was a psychiatrist in the US Army who taught me invaluable lessons about the family of man. The Carl Foreman of whom I speak was always nearby when I stumbled, as young men tend to do when indecision catches them between the promise of instant seductive pleasures and the discipline to postpone pleasure when values and

The Carl Foreman of whom I speak was always nearby when I stumbled, as young men tend to do when indecision catches them between the promise of instant seductive pleasures and the discipline to postpone pleasure when values and character require.

character require. Character is a quality found in some human beings. In Carl Foreman, without doubt, it was the essence of the man. Integrity, decency, and compassion also lived somewhere deep inside the man. The human being of whom I speak has touched most of us gathered here and has left us the better for it.

And I'm sure that includes our two award recipients as well, who will soon be heading for a closer look at the Hollywood that presently exists. We know that the old one that turned its back on Carl is no longer there. But the new one is far from problem-free. And not just a few of them are of its own making. I've been there almost forty-five years. I have tried to keep a watchful eye—and, indeed, I have seen a thing or two. In some ways what exists is better. In some ways it is only different. In some ways it is obviously worse than ever. It is also obvious that it has been good to me, and good for me. But remember, I went there with a back stiffened by character absorbed from all the Carl Foremans who have touched my life. Plus, I was lucky. And I wish the same for you. Luck, chance, serendipity, are major players in that town. And they do make a difference. If they take your arm, good things do happen.

But your destiny remains in your hands much of the way, since you are always hard at work in that regard long before luck, chance, and serendipity weigh in. Out of your imagination, through your fingers onto the page it must go—you and your talent alone at the spinning wheel. The story idea, the characters who populate it, how those characters interrelate with each other, how they grow, how they suffer, how they change is up to you. You create. The actor brings a face, the director brings a point of view, the producer brings casting suggestions, sometimes money, and always a nephew from the sausage business in Baltimore. But you bring the most important element of all: the script, the piece, the material. Your labor, your creation starts the process. And nothing can ever change that.

But be alert. The Hollywood that presently exists is not a Hollywood filled with Carl Foremans. In fact, I have yet to come upon another. It is a place where loyalty too often falls prey to expediency, where blame is a stepchild and success has many fathers. But don't be dismayed. You may be lucky and find a teacher, a Jewish waiter, or an army psychiatrist to lead you towards the light.

As we gather here in troubled times in a troubled world where spoken words seem to have lost their meaning, the language of the heart still speaks and the language of the soul responds, and you are, without question, better at the language of the heart and soul than anyone else in the process chain. So, journey onward to the town to see what you can see, learn what you can learn. And with a little luck, you will one day send them the message that the character of Carl Foreman still lives. And teach those willing to learn that a better, safer, healthier, violence-free world demands responsibility for all.

THE UNITED NEGRO COLLEGE FUND FREDERICK D. PATTERSON AWARDS DINNER

Frederick Douglass Patterson was a scholar of veterinary medicine before becoming the third president of the Tuskegee Institute in 1935, which under his leadership was greatly expanded to include graduate studies and new programs for engineering and aviation—the latter of which led to the establishment of a training site for military aircraft and a full US air base at Tuskegee. In 1944, he founded the United Negro College Fund (UNCF), which continues to support students through their college education. Sidney, who felt strongly about supporting education for the underserved, was honored by the UNCF in October 1998.

One by one a multitude of people have brushed by my life over these seventy-one years. Some have lingered only a magical moment; others tarried awhile longer before they moved on.

Each, without exception, left me richer in heart and mind. Now, tonight, I don't stand here alone. At my side in spirit and memory are those who have accompanied me across the years. Those who stood fast against the wind, so a little boy could learn early in his life what it means to persevere. Without them, I would be standing, or sitting, or lying down somewhere else tonight following another road.

Clearly, a time of reckoning is upon me. How do I say thank you to each of them to sufficiently cover my debt? Behind each deed of kindness was a face, a smile, another human being who cared enough to pause in their own journey to leave me a bit of the best of themselves. I will not try this evening to put in balance the indebtedness of this life of mine to that multitude that has nurtured, comforted, encouraged, and guided me all the way from my very first step to the one I've just taken to reach this podium. Time does not permit, and words will surely fall short.

But given the nature of my debt, I must—from this night on—make the most of the years I yet may spend. For therein lies the only way a proper "thank you" can be said to everyone, but especially to all those warriors who were with me in the trenches covering my ignorance, my innocence, and my back, giving me time to take hold, to strengthen my legs for the long run.

There were such warriors then, and there are such warriors now. My dear, loving, wonderful wife, Joanna, heads a special brigade with my six daughters and five grandchildren right behind. And behind them is a wealth of good friends—significantly more than any one man could hope for in a single lifetime.

It's said that when one begins being honored by dinners, salutes, and tributes, a wheelchair or a nursing home is sitting out of focus over there on the periphery. So just a word of caution to whom it may concern. Don't rush to give me no more dinners, and I never was that crazy about salutes and tributes anyhow.

I tell myself—and I take comfort in the thought—that my seventy-one years are only fractionally past the halfway mark, and I don't want nobody coming with no more dinners, no more salutes, no more tributes.

I share this evening with all those loving, unknown hands that have pushed me gently along the way, including those whose hands have left their mark on the world at large—and this old world, and me, are the better for it.

As I travel along life's road, moving steadily towards the sunset, I pause for a contemplative moment occasionally and review the years behind me. Spot-checking the pluses and minuses, in a sense. And I have come up with no more than a handful of regrets. Principal among which are: I regret the world getting better slower than I'd like. I regret, I have never beaten Bill Cosby at tennis. I regret I could never, try as I might, sing as well as [Harry Belafonte]. I regret public education has too few friends in high places. I regret where my varicose vein is located.

And, finally, I regret that the time limits of this program are such I cannot move around this room and hug each and every one of you for the wonderful show of support your presence here exhibits for the good work of the United Negro College Fund. For the moment, in the interest of time, please let a heartfelt "thank you" suffice. And, to the United Negro College Fund, I believe this nation is lucky to have you and will be luckier still when it matures to the place where the recognition of your true value will be common knowledge. I thank you.

THE COLLEGE OF THE BAHAMAS COMMENCEMENT

A proud Bahamian citizen, Sidney returned to the islands often and built a home there in the early 1970s, where he and Joanna lived for several years. He later became the Bahamian ambassador to Japan (1997-2007) and its ambassador to UNESCO (2002-2007). Today the bridge linking downtown Nassau to Paradise Island is named in his honor.

In June 1999 he spoke at the graduation ceremonies for the College of the Bahamas (now the University of the Bahamas). Like his other commencement addresses, Sidney elaborates on his own experience as a young boy on Cat Island who pulled himself up through hard work and dedication to find personal success, something he hopes that the graduates in the audience can similarly experience. By speaking directly to these young adults about the shoulders on which they stand, he cuts to the heart of his philosophy of gratitude for one's forebears and the importance of continued struggle for succeeding generations.

Sidney was very proud of his still young country, its having only gained independence from the United Kingdom in 1973, and he was hopeful for its future. He viewed the graduates and their college education as key ingredients in helping the nation continue down a prosperous and democratic path.

Certain passages of this speech were borrowed from his 1994 commencement address for Sarah Lawrence College (see page 146).

Thank you, President Higgs, honorable prime minister, distinguished members of government, young ladies and gentlemen of the graduating class, your compatriots in the continuing student body, faculty members, parents, and friends, I welcome you to this long-awaited, very good evening.

Your presence here speaks of quick minds, keen interest, vibrant curiosities, and expectations that threaten to keep me on my toes and make me reach beyond my grasp. Waiting to be introduced to you, I realized I was more than a little nervous. Because if you are, in fact, all those things—quick and curious and expectant—it means I will have to struggle to measure up, so that you won't have to measure down. I would hate that.

All in all, I am pressed by conscience to admit that when I first received your most generous invitation, I was troubled by the fact that I didn't really know the College of the Bahamas or the class of '99. To whom, therefore, would I speak? And what should I say? Should I speak to the graduating students, whom I didn't really know; or through the students to their parents, whom I likewise really didn't know; or though the parents to the larger community, where I do know a few people, from my early childhood days "over the hill" at Ross Corner and East Street. Most of whom have moved on to nicer times and better days. Many of whom are now grandparents of young men and women very much like you who make up the class of '99.

After some earnest wrestling with the question, I found the premise on which my response to the invitation would be based. I would speak only to you, the graduating class. Parents, friends, and faculty can listen if they choose, but my remarks, I decided, should be strictly from me directly to the class of '99.

As the world can see, you too are experiencing a little nervousness on this very good evening. Plus, you are flushed with anticipation for, and anxiety about, what tomorrow brings and brimming with relief that this day has finally arrived. But there is something about you that doesn't meet the eye, and it is that which has captured my interest. So let me begin by drawing your attention to a simple truth that sometimes goes unnoticed.

Long before you were born, there were men and women looking out for you. Men and women long since dead have left you many things, each of which was paid for with sweat, blood, and tears over many long years of very hard work. Their sacrifices, their pain, their struggles made it possible for you to be born in a free country. They spent themselves in a lifetime effort to leave you fruits they would never taste. Even the diploma you have earned from this great institution that validated the education you have received was not possible without some input from those who have been looking out for you—over generations past—before you were born. This institution and your education are gifts they had in mind that would one day be visited upon you.

Today, it would be safe to say that they are pleased to know that this institution, through that education, has armed you with weapons with which to face all the struggles of life that lie ahead. Critical thinking is now a part of your arsenal. The power of reason is now a part of your arsenal. Knowledge, imagination, creativity, perseverance, commitment to ancestors long gone, to try always to be a part of the solution and not part of the problem,

A steadfast champion for his home country, Sidney—seen here with Emperor Akihito—served as the Bahamian ambassador to Japan for a full decade.

is now a part of your arsenal. On the basis of these facts alone, all those who died before 1967 would now rest easier. Their personal message to you today would be this simple reminder: that these Bahama Islands are your home. And your home is a part of the world. And the world is moving fast. Their dearest hope is that you will keep pace with the speed of this modern world, the rhythm of it, the tempo of it, the politics of it, the economics of it, the danger of it, the complexity of it. They are confident in their expectation that you will become and remain conversant with all the forces that make this world go round. Your survival, our survival, the future of this now free, democratic country and the culture of its people depend on it—depend on your education.

To that simple truth let me add this personal thought: your assembly here,

today, creates in me a nostalgia that is overwhelming. Sixty years ago, I quietly dropped out of Western Senior School at the age of twelve and a half and went to work with a pick and shovel on what was then known as Hog Island—known to you today as Paradise Island. Our times are different. You are poised at the edge of new beginnings. You have just stepped into the starter's gate, just settled into the blocks, before you begin your run in the all-important race of your lives, the "preparedness stakes."

Sixty years ago was my generation's time at the edge of new beginnings. Today you are ready to take off, loaded with dreams that will fuel your journey across the sixty years ahead. After that, you will coast the rest of the way on wonderful memories collected over useful and productive lifetimes. But first, you have got to make it across those sixty years. It won't be easy, trust me. If you don't trust me, ask your parents. Or ask the prime minister. Or ask Ms. Keva Bethel. Or ask your grandparents, who are more than likely my age, and were more than likely standing at the edge of our generation's new beginning—loaded with dreams, and maybe a pick and shovel to start their journey.

Now with that said, let me speak a bit about fun. Having a good time, and about a place you've never been. A stimulating, tantalizing, seductive, intense place sitting just to the east of your imagination and west of your dreams. Fun, good times, enjoyment. Sounds like Hollywood, life in the fast lane. But you know, it's not. You know that Hollywood's disproportionate view of sex, drugs, violence, and assorted depravities is only a cheap distorted imitation. You know there is much more to the place I'm talking about than Hollywood has the courage to explore. The place of which I speak is, of course, "the real, real adult world," where there are no rewinds. Where one can't replay only the good times. Where there are no fast-forward buttons for skipping over the pain or leapfrogging the hard choices. You go through once. You get through once. That's life and that's real. But you know that, and you're not terrified by change. Therefore,

on this very good afternoon, as you are poised and ready to begin your journey on such beckoning, unknown roads as will pull at your curiosity, let us pause here for a word or two about what to expect.

Convictions firmly held will, somewhere along life's road, test your strength of character. So expect, therefore, to swim against the tide sometimes. Expect integrity, honesty, fairness, dignity, compassion, to be in evidence in all your undertakings. And question firmly, vigorously, the absence of any one of them. Make your word your bond. Expect to look that middle-aged man in the eyes and tell him "Thanks" for swimming as fast as he could, to keep you afloat. Expect to take Mom in your arms, share a tear, and let her know you appreciate it all.

Expect you may find a world that is not working quite as well as you feel it should, or would like it to. For the fact is the world at large is not in the best of shape at the moment. Expect to be welcomed into it because your ideas, your input, your energy, your dreams are essential to its future. Expect the unexpected—so hidden resistance from certain quarters that see you coming as successors, as replacements or competitors, won't throw you off stride for more than a second.

Expect to live out your lives in what will be a wonderful, remarkable country. To some of you, she may, from time to time, appear to have more flaws than you can comfortably acknowledge. But she will improve because of what you will demand of her and what she will have to deliver to you. But she can be the best there is and therefore deserves the best you have to give her. Expect to find love and romance and a healthy family life. And, at the proper time, we want you to have children of your own so you will know exactly where gray hairs come from. We owe you that one.

You have been a long time coming to this afternoon of appreciation for your accomplishments so far. You have worked hard and well. The books have been cracked, you have burned the midnight oil, you have taken tests, you have given answers. Written essays, researched subjects, and grades that had to be pulled up a notch or two or else, have been elevated. Everything is stamped "Mission Accomplished." All of it behind you, as you look ahead to the future, the new job, the new school, the new environment awaiting you. You have a sense, that on this special day, you can do no wrong because for so long you have done so much so right. An indisputable sense of accomplishment hovers above you. And the look in your eyes tells me that you are convinced that you have earned the right to cut loose this weekend, let your hair down and boogie. I am sure parents and friends will join me in saying amen to that—we are confident that it will be clean, hard, healthy fun.

Finally, be forewarned, and expect that it will fall to you and your generation to heal a world in which racial, religious, ethnic, and class hatreds vibrate and shimmer at subtle velocities constantly and, far too often, erupt into catastrophic convulsions, leaving scars, always leaving scars that disfigure the landscape of human life. Nothing escapes—not the politics, not the economics, not the arts, not you, not me, not the culture itself. They are not new racial, religious, ethnic, and class hatreds, and we do not yet understand them. Do they truly spring from some still unexplored place deep inside as from some native reservoir down at stat very core, outside the reach of our consciousness, where they defiantly bide their time unimpressed with our efforts to define them? And explain them? And hopefully correct them? We are sorry to say, as we pass you a world in which such questions remain unanswered, at least for most of the human family, that logic and reason vigorously applied have not yet broken them down in understandable terms for us. And now, with our generation's time running low, it falls to you to keep an eye on these scourges and never let the demons feeding at their roots wander out of sight. And, please make note, to our credit, that it was not for want of trying on our part that such unfinished business and such dangerous, unanswered questions are left to you.

Our efforts were often well intended, constant, and firm, but not enough. Racial, religious, and ethnic hatreds still blaze fiercely in too many places on the globe, in spite of our considerable energies to the contrary. If a suggestion on the point is permissible before you accept the reins of a world so inexplicably flawed, an occasional unblinking look into the dark side of human nature may be a useful addition to your efforts. It could be that the clearest views of demons can be had by observation of the area where they dwell. And don't be too surprised to find racism, anti-Semitism, sexism, and homophobia living somewhere in that same neighborhood—right next door, most likely. It is only a suggestion, and one that comes from an uncomfortable sense that too many of our generation in the world at large didn't look hard enough or long enough inside themselves. If your reach does not exceed your grasp, then what's a heaven for?

As I stand here looking at you, I believe there are future doctors in this room. And more than a few future lawyers. There are future businessmen and -women heading for considerable success—sitting in this auditorium at this very moment. Future scientists, future engineers, future accountants, future educators, future artists, and computer experts are also present here. In this class of '99—including those who have made note of all the shameful errors of grammar I have subjected them to in the course of my remarks—I offer my apology for such shortcomings on condition that you never forget . . .

There are no shortcuts for the doctor nor the lawyer, nor the scientist, nor the engineer, nor the architect, nor any of the other professions you aspire to. You are just moments away from becoming like me, like your dad, like your mom, adults. Your passport in that real, real world, throughout your life, will be your education.

Your education will give you something to sell. At the foundation of this entire world, you will find commerce is one of its most important cornerstones. And therefore, the quality of your adult lives will depend on what you have to sell that is necessary and useful to the lives of other people. Doctors sell health care to keep us well, and they do pretty nicely, let me tell you. Lawyers sell their knowledge of the law, which enables them access to such things as are necessary to a good material life.

Scientists, businessmen, inventors, engineers, architects, specialists of a hundred different varieties, and professionals of every kind, too numerous to itemize here, all have enviable material lifestyles because their education has given them something to sell that is necessary and useful in the lives of people throughout the nation and, in most cases, throughout the world.

"Money does not grow on trees." My mother, like many mothers, has said that a thousand times. When you are an adult and on your own, if you have nothing to sell you will also have little with which to buy. That is the way of the world, and that is basic. But however important money may be, there are more important values in life—and your education will lead you to both money and the necessary human values to nurture and strengthen our community.

But all through your early years, before you arrived at this moment of your new beginning, nature has decreed that you grow towards it day by day, bit by bit, over a continuing period of time, until you became ready to assume full membership, full responsibility in it. In the meantime, nature arranged that someone else had to do the swimming or you would sink. Someone else had to play the survival game—and win—or you would have perished. Fact of the matter is, you were in on a pass. And thanks to nature, you were connected by a bond of love as old and as strong as nature itself.

Until you could pay your own rent, buy your own food, pull your own weight, pay for your own keep, a middle-aged guy somewhere out there with a little gray at his temple had to stay in the water, swimming as fast as he could. Mom had to play steady at the survival game and dare not lose. But you are only moments from ready, only moments before you will be shouldering your own survival responsibilities, and one day soon you'll be doing your own swimming, and that middle-aged guy can take a rest, and Mom can ease up and kick back and give a little more of her time to herself.

Therefore, in closing, allow me a moment or two for a word or two about the fathers who have been swimming as fast as they could all these years to keep you afloat, and for the moms who had to play steady at the survival game and win or you would have perished. I believe the proud parents in this room feel that they are sending forth the best of themselves out into the world or to institutions of higher learning. And if what I have seen here today is an example, then Mom and Dad have been helped considerably in their achievement by good and caring teachers and the wonderful administration of the College of the Bahamas.

I am probably the person who has learned the most as a result of your most generous invitation. I see that a great nation is made up, in large measure, of small communities with steadfast values and decent, hardworking, ordinary human beings like the College of the Bahamas community of families. To the class of '99, the "that" about you that doesn't readily meet the eye, and which has captured my interest is that intangible force inside you with which nature stamps you as having the courage and the curiosity to travel those beckoning unknown roads that lie just to the east of the imagination and west of your dreams.

Thank you for your hospitality. I applaud the moms and dads for being there for you and being here with you. I salute the College of the Bahamas community of families for their dedication and commitment, and I congratulate you, young men and women, who will go on from here to light the way. Thank you.

THE NATIONAL CIVIL RIGHTS MUSEUM

The National Civil Rights Museum was constructed around the former Lorraine Motel in Memphis, Tennessee, the site of the 1968 assassination of Martin Luther King Jr. It was one of the first civil rights museums in America when it opened in 1991, and it has annually presented the Freedom Award to individuals whose work has made an impact "in the name of freedom and civil rights." Sidney was named an honoree in 2001 alongside Óscar Arias, the former president of Costa Rica. Here, he speaks to a young audience whose ancestors—honored by the museum—laid the foundation for their future success.

In the early 1950s and '60s, when the civil rights movement was struggling to be heard against monumental resistance, it seemed the overwhelming majority of the nation's population didn't think that such a reality as civil rights for us would, or should, ever come to be. Their vote was registered against equal access to education for us, against equal access to housing for us, against equal access to job opportunities for us, and, as history has recorded, against equal access to those civil rights, those civil liberties, those protections under the law—all of which were guaranteed by the Constitution of the United States of America to all its citizens, except to us and nearly all other people of color. That is how it was forty, fifty, sixty years ago—in a time different than we now know. Therefore, it was not expected that African American young men and young women would soon set out with an unshakable resolve—to change the course of American history—by letting it be known that they were coming to engage racism on every level, in every walk of life. Coming with an unconquerable determination to do battle, until every member of their community—everywhere—could sit or stand, as we are doing here today, under the full reach of civil laws, rules and regulations, rights and privileges, backed by the total power of the Constitution of these United States to include every citizen in every state.

The young men and young women of the African American community—true to their promise that they would come, strong in the conviction that that which is wrong,

unjust, inhumane, and ungodly will not, must not, cannot be allowed to stand—they came, as they promised they would, to address the unfinished business of a nation's most unworthy deeds. High among which was standing shamelessly on ethical and moral ground in defense of the indefensible. Those young African Americans had come on behalf of themselves, their parents, their forefathers and mothers, and the history of the African American people.

Sidney in 1960 with Civil Rights icons Martin Luther King Jr., Harry Belafonte, and labor leader A. Philip Randolph

For me it was in the early 1940s when I, too, was one of America's children. I recall it now as a time when the burdens of age-appropriate responsibilities were resting heavily on the shoulders of children of color— even the very, very young.

This afternoon, as I look around, I can see among the many faces gathered here those of the young—ten years old, twelve years old, fourteen years old. Some of you are three generations removed from the time of which I speak.

Therefore, it is only natural that you would wonder what could you possibly have in common with an old guy like me. You see me standing here, looking like I'm just about to plop over, and you're thinking, "He even looks older than my grandfather—and my grand is old, creaky bones and everything." Truth is, I'm probably older than your great-grandfather. Fact is, I'm hoping you were brought here today by your grandfather or your great-grandfather. If so, by now you're probably thinking you're surrounded by old creaky guys, and if grandma is also along, we've really got you boxed in. You're trapped, and you're thinking to yourself, you're not gonna like having to listen to a lot of old-time, ancient stuff about how things were in the olden days, before you were even born and stuff. Well, it is not now and never has been my intent to trap you—but if that's the way you feel, maybe we can cut a deal advantageous to us both.

Would you endure a few minutes of feeling trapped? In exchange for one of life's most valuable lessons? That can be used as a key to open many doors? If you agree, I promise to only intrude on your attention just long enough to remind you of a few things we do have in common. The most important

and priceless of which is that we are bound together. You, your mom and dad, their moms and dads, and their moms and their dads— four generations of your family are all bound together—as are you and I—by a common history. There are thousands of generations who have gone before you with whom you share a common history. And every generation was made up of the young like you and the old like me. A thousand years ago there were young girls who looked like you—were as pretty as you—and young boys of eight and ten and twelve and fourteen who were as handsome and as manly as you. They lived in a different place, in a different time than you, but you share the same history. Because history is shared by all the people who make it.

Our African American history is shared with the African people. And the African people's history goes back to the very beginning of mankind. In fact, it is generally accepted among archaeologists, historians, scientists, and educators everywhere that Africa was the birthplace of all mankind; men, women, boys, and girls everywhere in the family of man originated in Africa. In the beginning, human beings existed in groups of communally interdependent units, now called tribes. And some of those tribes—over millions and millions of years—slowly, of their own free will, wandered off into other parts of the earth. Some wandered into what is now called Asia. Some wandered north of what is now called the Sahara Desert, and still others continued on into the cold climates, now called Europe. Some of them eventually wandered—also of their own free will—into other portions of the earth now called the Americas.

Then, many thousands of years later, tribes from north of the desert and out of the cold countries returned to the birthplace of the human race and forced descendants of the earliest tribes onto ships that transported them—against their will—away from their ancestral home and delivered them, under duress, into captivity, subjugation, and servitude.

"Under duress." "Duress" was often used as a polite word for slavery. But you and I know there is no polite word for slavery.

I know you're thinking: "Why is this old guy telling us all this old-fashioned stuff when we could be boogying, jamming, slamming, and dancing 'the hot slinky low down and dirty' that drives parents and other grown-ups nuts? They totally don't get it! Grown-ups totally don't get it!" Right? Well, listen—your few minutes are not up yet. You're still trapped, and there's nothing you can do about it. Because Grandpa and/or Grandma is there, and either one will kick your butt. So just lay back and cool it!

These few minutes might change your life. Because knowing your own history puts you within striking distance of knowing yourself. Knowing the history of a thing, a place, a circumstance, a person, a people, provides you with the information necessary to deal effectively in your own interest with that thing, that place, that circumstance, that person, those people—whoever they may be. If you know the history of the world, you then know that the world is moving fast—and therefore you know, then, that you need the necessary information that will allow you to fix yourself in time and not let the world get so far ahead of you that you can't catch up. If you don't know the history of information, then you won't know that information transforms into education. If you don't know the history of education, then you won't understand that education transforms into knowledge. And if you don't know the history of knowledge, then you won't be aware that knowledge—on rare occasions—does transform into wisdom. If you don't know the history of wisdom, you won't know all the reasons why Grandpa and Grandma are the remarkable people that they are. Through all of their life's experiences, their survival depended on the kind of information they could gather, the amount of education they could wrestle out of a system that was not always education-friendly to them, their culture, or their history. Their survival depended on the degree of knowledge they could extract from such education as was grudgingly available to them. Out of little or nothing they have created for you a world better than they had. Their lives have set a rock-solid example for you to remember where they came from, and where they expect you to go. They're confident in the knowledge that you fully understand that without information you won't know where to start, without education and knowledge the world becomes a blur—life becomes a perpetual confrontation with the unknown. You and your history will lose your power in the eyes of other people's information, education, and knowledge. The value of our history must be evident in the purpose of our lives.

So I have tried to make it plain to see that—for you, the young who would like to go boogying right now, and me, an old guy with creaky bones and stuff—we do have a few things in common. My bones are creaky

> *Throughout your life's journey you must seek out and strike up an acquaintance with ambition, opportunity, motivation, critical thinking, self-application, and curiosity.*

partly because I have already traveled most of this long road of life while you, with the young, sturdy bones of youth, are preparing for the start of your journey along that same road of life, which now lies ahead of you.

Allow me, this old guy with creaky bones and stuff, to leave you with a gift of value. Names. Names that have no faces. Through-

out your life's journey you must seek out and strike up an acquaintance with ambition, opportunity, motivation, critical thinking, self-application, and curiosity. Where would you find them? Big question.

Let's start with ambition. That one is not so hard to come by. Early in life we start catching glimpses of it, streaking on the out-skirts of our imagination. And soon, as early as five or six, we notice it making occasional appearances in our daydreams. And as we grow older, we run across it in other places. Maybe down the block at a cousin's house, maybe on the corner while we are hanging loose with friends, laughing and joking with each other—about girls if you are a boy; about boys if you are a girl. Or maybe you've seen it in a movie or read in a book, or recognized it in a teacher, or a minister, or a businessman, or a doctor, or a factory worker, or a mother, or a father in the house of that cousin down the block. From early times we were able to recognize ambition at work even though we couldn't call it by name.

And what about the others—opportunity, motivation, critical thinking, self-application, and curiosity? Where would we find them? Big question indeed! Because such life as we can have, by our own hands, our own efforts, and our own will, cannot be fashioned with-out them. God and nature will assist, to be sure. But the life we want, and feel that we deserve, must be designed and constructed by us as individuals. Not our fathers, not our mothers, and not our cousin who lives in the house down the block. But us—me in my case, you in yours. Opportunity seldom comes looking for us. It is almost always the other way around. The hand of opportunity is usually won by suitors who diligently go in search of her affections. Certainly, that seems to have been the case throughout most of human history. If one does not go out in search of opportunity, one might never lay eyes upon its face. And consequently, over time, one will grow resentful of those who have made the effort and have, therefore, been smiled upon for so doing. If our forefathers could speak, I believe they would strongly recommend that we keep sharp our ability to recognize opportunity, keep an eye out for her always. Check from time to time to make sure she's not sitting right under your nose unnoticed. Monitor her activities, track her whereabouts, keep notes on how often she smiles on people with high ambition drive, position yourself to run into her, and always be prepared to put your best foot forward and introduce yourself. Motivation fuels critical thinking, which encourages and strengthens self-application. Finally, without curiosity in the vanguard of our journey we will surely never travel very far. That is the best of all the gifts this old guy with creaky bones can leave you. It is my hope that when you have grown old and your bones have grown creaky, you will pass this lesson on to the very young before they go out to boogie and do their version of the slinky low down and dirty—that will drive you nuts! Remember, what goes around comes around.

My heartfelt thanks and appreciation to each of you for your presence here today. Likewise, to the Civil Rights Museum for their most generous invitation.

FULFILLMENT FUND STARS BENEFIT GALA

Sidney was a longtime supporter of Fulfillment Fund, a Los Angeles nonprofit that supports underprivileged youth in pursuit of a college education. The organization was founded in 1977 by Dr. Gary Gitnick—a UCLA physician and Sidney's doctor during his last thirty years—and his wife, Cherna Gitnick, as a mentoring program for children with disabilities. A longtime supporter of the organization, Sidney was honored with the Founder's Humanitarian Award at the Fulfillment Fund Stars Benefit Gala in Beverly Hills in October 2013. In his address, Sidney speaks of his own past and the importance of aiding other young people in their educational pursuits because of the help he himself had received.

Many years ago, I was invited to an evening centered around the magical powers of education—an evening that instantly befuddled me. I had, at that point in life, no idea of the fundamentals of education— the usefulness of it, the unknown power of it—hidden away outside the reach of my consciousness.

My parents were tomato farmers. Their children were five boys and three girls. Life was difficult for us all. I was the youngest, but life was not easy across the board. I had to go out and search for a paying job at the age of twelve.

At fifteen, I wound up in New York as a dishwasher in a small restaurant in Queens, Long Island. I was on my own—my choices were to survive or die.

I survived. I learned how to teach myself to learn, and I made a conscious effort to approach every day, striving to be better, to do better. But there were people, divine human beings, along the way who, out of sheer kindness, opened their hearts and made a difference in my life. Such was the case early on, in New York City, when I was arrested for vagrancy.

I was sixteen, destitute, no place to stay. It was in the dead of winter, and in an effort to stay warm, I found myself sleeping on the benches in the waiting room of the Penn Station railway terminal.

I was arrested, eventually, and taken into custody by two cops who held me until fingerprint records turned up nothing.

As I stepped out of the door of that police station, one of the white officers in that precinct followed me onto the street and asked, "Where will you go?" I said, "I don't know, I really don't know." That officer then reached in his pocket and gave me fifty cents and said, "There's an orphanage in Brooklyn run by Catholic sisters—I think they will take you in." He wrote down the address. I thanked him for the fifty cents and the suggestion. I went to Brooklyn. The sisters took me in and treated me well, with genuine love and affection.

They helped me with time enough to get my bearings—time enough to put on my thinking cap—and come up with a reasonable survival tactic against the ravages of winter. Within two weeks, I left the Catholic sisters with my gratitude for their kindness.

I am also reminded of a Jewish waiter I met in Queens while working in a small restaurant as a dishwasher. At closing time one evening, while I waited for him and his fellow waiters to finish their coffee and leave so I could wash the last few dishes—he saw me sitting in the dining room, near the entrance to the kitchen, trying as best I could at reading a newspaper. He wandered over to where I was sitting and asked me what was new in the papers. It was an uncomfortable feeling for me, but I answered it truthfully. I told him I was trying to teach myself to read better and that I couldn't really explain what was going on in the papers because I hadn't had very much education. He offered to read the paper with me. I accepted. Every night that followed, while his fellow waiters were having their coffee and snacks before taking off for home, he sat with me—weeks on end—and helped me learn to read better.

Later in life, I would regret not having jotted down his family's name—or that of the police officer. I owe them both, and many others, so much. Their compassion took precedence in moments when it could have been so easy to look the other way. Instead, they lent a hand. And I am forever grateful for their humanity.

Gary and Cherna Gitnick and everyone gathered here this evening speaks loudly of the oneness of the human spirit. It is out of that oneness that the Fulfillment Fund was created thirty-six years ago by Gary and Cherna. And this wonderful organization has done for many what the police officer and the waiter did for me. This organization has shown young men and young women wanting to do better—striving for a better life—that despite life's twists and turns, they matter. And that with hard work, they can have better.

I extend my deepest thanks to the Fulfillment Fund board and to Gary and Cherna Gitnick for this distinguished award and honor. Joanna and I, and our family, owe so

Fulfillment Fund founder Dr. Gary Gitnick with Sherri Poitier, Sydney Poitier, and their father

much to these two exceptional human beings who, despite having full and demanding lives, could not bring themselves to look the other way.

It was on their backs, and the backs of so many others dedicated to educating our youth, that this evening was built, and on behalf of American education and all of America's children, we are all the better for having them rally on our behalf and on the behalf of mankind.

I am often reminded that the number of human creatures on this small planet we call home is now seven billion. The challenges awaiting humankind are huge, and it is ultimately up to everyone here to lend a hand in educating the children of the world to lead mankind to far better worlds than we, sitting here now, can possibly imagine.

The brilliant young men and women recognized this evening are the trailblazers of that quest, making sure that empathy and compassion continue to travel alongside curiosity and knowledge as they forge ahead, searching for the answers to unknown questions.

Thank you all for your time and attention, and may we continue to educate and nurture our children so that our children's children will lead us to other worlds yet unknown.

I HAVE OFTEN WONDERED WHAT A[...]
RIT ONCE IT HAS BEEN RELEASED FRO[...]
IS WORLD OF MATERIAL MATTER.
[TH]OUGHTS, I HAVE PONDERED THE QUES[...]
[...]NG AND NEVER MORE INTENSELY AS WH[...]
[F]RIEND OR A RESPECTED ACQUAINTAN[...]
[...]OM US AND ONTO THAT ETERNAL JOURNEY.

I BELIEVE NOW, AS IN THE CASE OF
[...]E CHARACTER OF THE MAN IS INSEPA[...]
[...]RIT. HIS INTEGRITY AND HIS WORD
[...]KEWISE TRAVELING COMPANIONS TO [...]
[...]LY MEMORIES THAT CAN LAST FOREVER
[...]AT ONCE WARMED HIS NOW STILLED [...]

RICHARD PRYOR - DGA TRIBUTE -

[...]ness, creative instinct walks a long, lonel[y]

[...]sion it falters, we taste of defeat.

[...]ys steadfast and true, it brings us to mo[...]

[...]es are in order and a collective "thank-you" [...]

[...]us, nature has assigned modest tools—

[...]we must try to chisel, inch by inch—

[...]d productive path through life.

[...]s in the hands of most of us, barely managed
[...]et the job done -- even modestly.

[...]our tools and ourselves were insufficient to

[...]on the other hand, there was Richard Pryor—

[...]assigned modest tools like the rest of us.

[...]e to load him up you with a great talent[...]

BROCK PETERS
MEMORIAL

FOR SOME OF US THE WORLD WILL BE
FRACTIONALLY IMBALANCED FOR A LITTLE WHILE.
THEN IT WILL CORRECT ITSELF, AS IT ALWAYS HAS.

IN THE PROCESS--AS ALWAYS--FAMILY MEMBERS,
FRIENDS-
ACQUAINTANCES-
AND ADMIRERERS-

WILL FACE THE MANY DIFFICULT, BUT NECESSARY,
ADJUSTMENTS THAT INEVITABLY ARISE-
WHEN SOMEONE SO LOVED, SO RESPECTED, SO
ADMIRED GOES AWAY.

BUT- OUR RESTORATIVE POWERS-
LIKE ~~THE~~ THAT BEING WORLD'S-
WILL KICK IN--AND WE WILL

MAKE THE MANY DIFFICULT AJUSTMENTS
NECESSARY TO HOLD THE LIFE OF ~~(THE DEPARTED~~ ^AChristine Smith
~~LOVED ONE)~~ IN OUR EMBRACE FOREVER.
Who WAS This DEPARTED LOVEeD ONE For whom WEHAV[E]
GATHERED HERE TO BRING A FINAL GOOD [...] SHE WAS MA[NY]
Things TO MANY OF US, SHE WAS WIFE TO ME A MOTHER TO HER SON, A WIFE
TO HER HUSBAND, GRANDMOTHER TO HER GRANDCHILDREN A
WHO IS THIS ACTOR, THIS SINGER, THIS
PRODUCER, ~~THIS LECTURER,~~ THIS DOER OF GOOD
Who CONSTANTLY TRIED TO LIFT ~~ENTER~~ THE BURDENS OF LIFE ~~ON THE~~ WHEN EV[ER]
NAMED BROCK PETERS? ~~...~~ THEY FALL ON THE BACKS OF
FAMILY MEMBERS, FRIENDS OR NEIGHBORS
SIXTY YEARS AGO, BROCK PETERS, WILLIAM
GREAVES, EARL HYMAN, CHARLIE BLACKWELL,
WILLIAM MARSHALL, JULIAN MAYFIELD, JAMES
EDWARDS, THE INCOMPARABLE ROSCO LEE BROWN,
IVAN DIXON AND MYSELF—
EACH HAD CHOSEN TO BECOME ACTORS IN THE
AMERICAN THEATRE.

MEMORIALS

We love; we work; we raise our families.
Those are the areas of significance in our individual lives.
And love and work and family are the legacy we leave
behind when our little moment in the sun is gone.

—The Measure of a Man

C lose personal relationships came naturally to Sidney, and he was by many accounts a generous and gracious friend to others in his life. Having worked in Hollywood for decades—and on the New York stage before that—he crossed paths with many talented artists and formed, in some cases, lifelong connections. It goes without saying that he was also a significant public figure whom others wanted to know and work with, and as an affable spokesman for the film industry, he was often called upon to memorialize friends and colleagues who had passed away.

The following section contains eulogies and excerpts from tributes to those who made an impact in Sidney's life and art, and in addition to acknowledging debts owed and gratitude for those who paved the way for him, or those who worked with or for him, they express his insider's view of some of the most significant voices and personalities in Hollywood.

DOROTHY DANDRIDGE

A few months before becoming the first African American woman to be nominated for the Best Actress Oscar for *Carmen Jones*, Dorothy Dandridge attended an event in Harlem publicizing the 1954 film. Sidney first encountered her there, a moment that he recalls in his remarks below. The two would later work together on the turbulent set of *Porgy and Bess* (1959), which reunited her with her former director and lover, Otto Preminger. When the tyrannical Preminger treated her recklessly during filming, Sidney came to her defense and watched over her throughout the film's production. The celebrated actress passed away, too young, in 1965.

I first saw her walking into the ballroom of the Theresa Hotel at 125th Street and Seventh Avenue in New York City. Her carriage was regal; her smile was devastating. Her overall impact on the media and the several hundred people invited there to meet her was unforgettable. That evening, before I met her, I thought her a likely candidate for the most beautiful woman in the world. After I met her, I discovered there was more beauty yet hidden away behind that smile. Behind that devastating smile were personality treasures galore, more than most of us would be privileged to see in the few short years that were left to her.

During the *Porgy and Bess* shoot, "I learned that the serene look Dorothy Dandridge always wore only served to mask the fears, frustrations, and insecurities that were tumbling around inside her all the time," wrote Sidney in *This Life*.

"The love affair of this oddly-assorted pair has considerable humanity, though Dandridge is perhaps too refined to be quite convincing as the split-skirt, heroin-sniffing tramp," wrote *Variety* in its 1959 review of *Porgy and Bess*. OPPOSITE: In its review of *Uptown Saturday Night* (1974), the *New York Times* noted, "Mr. Poitier has had the good sense to hire a lot of exceptionally talented and funny people."

Having worked closely with that vulnerable, strong yet fragile, warm, down-to-earth, sometimes delicate, sometimes raucous personality, I can tell you that she was more a star than the circumstances of her time could make room for.

Question as we might Nature's reasons for the brevity of Dorothy's presence among us, it is better for us all to have known here for a short time than not to have known her at all. She was a leading lady in the truest sense of the word—and I'll miss her as long as I live.

RICHARD PRYOR

Sidney directed pioneering Black comedian and actor Richard Pryor in two commercial hits: *Uptown Saturday Night* (1974) and *Stir Crazy* (1980). Known for his edgy content and envelope-pushing style but troubled by substance abuse during this period, Pryor reportedly behaved well around Sidney, even if his energy was a challenge to contain on set. Pryor passed away in 2005.

In our business, creative instinct walks a long, lonely line, daily. On the occasion it falters, we taste of defeat. When it stays steadfast and true, it brings us to moments like these, when tributes are in order and a collective "thank you" is loudly proclaimed. To most of us, nature has assigned modest tools with which we must try to chisel, inch by inch, a useful and productive path through life. Modest tools in the hands of most of us barely managed sometimes to get the job done—even modestly.

Sometimes, our tools and ourselves were insufficient to the task. Sometimes, on the other hand, there was Richard Pryor, who wasn't assigned modest tools like the rest of us. Nature chose to load him up you with a great talent, impeccable timing, raw candor,

Sidney directed Richard Pryor and Gene Wilder in the popular comedy *Stir Crazy* (1980). The two comedians had previously appeared together in the hit film *Silver Streak* (1976).

a boyish smile, and a presence that seduced us instantly. However, nature did temper her generosity by giving him a short fuse. And, like the rest of us, it is fair to say, when he got pissed, he got pissed. But that, most of the world already knows.

He will leave an indelible mark on American culture, the motion picture industry, and wherever else great comedic talent will forever be held in high esteem. I know—I was witness to his genius. I experienced it firsthand. There will never be another Richard Pryor.

BROCK PETERS

Stage and screen actor Brock Peters is perhaps best known to audiences as the wrong-fully accused defendant Tom Robinson in the 1962 adaptation of *To Kill a Mockingbird* and was often cast by Hollywood producers as a stereotypical Black villain—including in the films *Carmen Jones* and *Porgy and Bess*, opposite Sidney and Dorothy Dandridge. Peters died in 2005.

Certain passages were first used in a 2001 memorial speech to director Stanley Kramer (see page 104). Similarly, Sidney would reuse the opening lines below in a trib-ute to talent agent Freddie Fields in 2007 (see page 86). He also borrows a line from Shakespeare at the conclusion. This recycling of material should not be read as a lack of effort on Sidney's part; the repeated praise is indicative of the artistry and coura-geous spirit of the people with whom he consistently surrounded himself.

For some of us the world will be frac-tionally imbalanced for a little while. Then it will correct itself, as it always has.

In the process—as always—family mem-bers, friends, acquaintances, and admirers will face the many difficult, but necessary, adjust-ments that inevitably arise when someone so loved, so respected, so admired goes away.

But our restorative powers, like the world's, will kick in—and we will make the many difficult adjustments necessary to hold the life of the departed loved one in our embrace forever.

Who is this actor, this singer, this pro-ducer, this lecturer, this doer of good named Brock Peters? Sixty years ago, Brock Peters, William Greaves, Earl Hyman, Charlie Black-well, William Marshall, Julian Mayfield, James Edwards, the incomparable Roscoe Lee Brown, Ivan Dixon, and myself each had cho-sen to become actors in the American theatre.

Some of us became writers instead, some of us became directors instead, some of us didn't make it. The luck of the draw eventu-ally turned their interests to other pursuits, elsewhere. As one among the survivors, I can tell you: Brock Peters took the high road through his entire life—to victory sometimes, to defeat sometimes—but always accepted responsibility for the choices that took him

A longtime advocate for Black artists and entertainers, Peters opined in *Variety* in December 1967 that white America "can accept only one successful Negro in each field at a time"—a reference to Sidney's dominance in Hollywood.

to either place. His biographical material and credits hint—only hint—at the awesome stature of the artist they suggest.

I know as a fact that the courage of this man has made a better man of me.

The Hollywood of Brock Peters's youth was not a courageous place. Nor was it a hospitable place for young men like himself, perceived as different enough to be viewed as trespassers, prowling too close to the edges of some private domain, near which they did not belong.

The Hollywood of Brock Peters's youth and mine contained striking similarities. At roughly the same time, we were both on the margins of the American social reality, for vastly different reasons. He was coming with ideas ahead of the times, and I was coming without credentials—a trespasser hoping to plead his case. Each heading in different directions, on different missions. Still, for reasons unknown, out paths were fated to cross. I would eventually be privileged to accompany him from time to time on short stretches of his journey—long enough to witness the moment-to-moment transformation his purpose would bring to bear on the Hollywood we knew. It seems to me that courage of a special kind came to visit on the heels of his arrival here. And while it stayed and roamed the town in low profile for years on end, it often was reminded to be careful where it stepped—and be watchful of its tongue.

Such image as courage now has in the Hollywood of today is owed in no small measure to the handful of men like Brock Peters, Ossie Davis, James Earl Jones—men who stood fast on difficult days and aligned themselves four-square with the values by which they conducted their lives as men, as husbands, as fathers, as citizens, and as artists. Men who came to town with expectations, men who arrived fully ready to accept as a given that they would have to swim against the tide sometimes.

The life's work of Brock Peters is a testament to courage, to integrity, to honesty, and to determination. Had he and his African American compatriots not elected to swim against the tide when the currents were sometimes at their strongest, the world would not have had the opportunity to experience the cinematic impact of their talents and their values—both of which added grace and a noticeable amount of humanity to the American film industry over the last fifty years. And during that time, he was a true friend.

And in my views and feelings, he will forever remain a fearless, courageous, multitalented American artist, worthy of the accolades, high praises, and awards the American theatre and the American film industry correctly—and proudly—register in his name. Brock Peters, a man among men. Farewell—for now—and may flights of angels sing thee to thy rest.

SPENCER TRACY

Sidney famously starred with Spencer Tracy and Katharine Hepburn in *Guess Who's Coming to Dinner* (1967), which was completed less than a month before Tracy's death at age sixty-seven. In 1986, Hepburn produced a tribute documentary, *The Spencer Tracy Legacy*, which premiered at a benefit for the American Academy of Dramatic Arts, an event that also marked the establishment of the Spencer Tracy Endowment Fund for Student Scholarships. Hepburn, Sidney, Robert Wagner, Stanley Kramer, and Frank Sinatra each spoke that evening, memorializing the legendary actor.

Spencer Tracy the actor, with his artistically exceptional body of work, had captured my allegiance years before I met Spencer Tracy the person—which was on an evening when Katharine Hepburn cooked dinner for me, Stanley Kramer, and Spencer Tracy at his home in Hollywood. With all due respect to Miss Hepburn's cooking, I don't recall the specifics of the meal, but I do recall every word said, every gesture made, and every pearl of wisdom dropped that evening. Studio press releases and gossip column tidbits had primed me to expect a roustabout, gung-ho, happy-go-lucky, hard-living fellow who was quite capable of losing a weekend from time to time. I found instead a man whose values fired his passion. A man bright, extremely well read, a philosophically well-rounded man who would probably raise

his fists to fight if someone called him an intellectual. But that is what was clearly his favorite chair. Miss Hepburn sat on the floor with her elbow on his knees. She had probably heard each story dozens of times before, but she was looking up at him the entire time, like a smitten seventeen-year-old. Eyes sparkling, she kept encouraging him to tell more stories. I knew, too, that the evening was meant to look me over, check me out, see what I was all about before filming began. I was a little apprehensive, because I had heard Miss Hepburn was not known for biting her tongue. That, I would later come to realize, was a gross understatement.

But never in my travels anywhere have I felt more at home than in the company of fellow actor Spencer Tracy. I have put him down among a very small group—a handful of actors

that I, as an actor, use as a reference point for excellence. Without question, Spencer Tracy's career could serve as a textbook for the craft.

One other thing I want to pass on to you: Miss Hepburn has long been known as a feisty, unbridled, untamed, shoot-from-the-hip lady. Well, he had her number. Around him she was a little pussycat. I swear, I don't know how he did it. But I will testify in court, that is the way it was. During the filming of

Sidney had earlier agreed to star opposite Tracy in *The Devil at 4 O'Clock* (1961), a big-budget adventure film from Columbia, but the deal fell apart. The role was ultimately played by Frank Sinatra.

Guess Who's Coming to Dinner, when they were both on the soundstage at the same time, you never heard a peep out of her. Not a peep. But whenever he wasn't around—boy! Oh boy! Oh boy! That, as much as anything else, speaks to the kind of fellow Spencer Tracy was.

PAUL WINFIELD

Paul Winfield was an Actors Studio member and celebrated stage actor before being recruited by Poitier for two of his earliest screen appearances: *The Lost Man* (1969) and *Brother John* (1971). For his lead performance in *Sounder* (1972), Winfield received an Oscar nomination for Best Actor. He went to on to more memorable roles on film and television, and passed away in 2004.

I have often wondered what accompanies the spirit once it has been released from life here, in this world of material matter. In my private thoughts, I have pondered the question hard and long and never more intensely as when a loved one, a friend, or a respected acquaintance steps away from us and onto that eternal journey.

I believe now, as in the case of Paul Winfield, the character of the man is inseparable from his spirit. His integrity and his word of honor are likewise traveling companions to his spirit, and only memories that can last forever—such as those that once warmed his now stilled heart—will be allowed to warm his spirit's passage into eternity.

Eternity lies beyond the physical universe; we all know that. Even the distance just to the center of the Milky Way galaxy, if traveled at the speed of light—186,000 miles per second—would take thirty thousand years.

Clearly, God has made our spirits infinitely tougher than he made the bodies in which he housed them for the short period he needed us in this material world.

One hundred eighty-six thousand miles per second for thirty thousand years, still the journey continues. A million years and onward still. A billion years. Fifteen billion years at the speed of 186,000 miles per second and yet eternity beyond. But God has yet to make a spirit that wasn't up to the distance. My mother has made it. My father, brothers and sisters, friends and respected acquaintances. And now, Paul Winfield—brother, friend, and highly respected fellow artist—has also arrived. He's already there. Don't try to calculate the distance covered. Those numbers are only useful here, in this material world. Over there, God has shortcuts to get his spirits home.

So, Pat, be at ease in your mind and in your heart. Let your grief face the sun and

open yourself to as full and meaningful a life as you can possibly have. I count your brother Paul among the stars—not only here on earth but in the heavens as well.

After *Sounder*, Winfield and Cicely Tyson costarred in other projects, including the acclaimed television miniseries *King* (1978).

FREDDIE FIELDS

Joanna Poitier's agent, Freddie Fields, co-founded the talent agency Creative Management Associates in 1960 and was the mastermind behind First Artists, a production company run by Sidney, Paul Newman, Barbra Streisand, and others in the late 1960s. He later became an independent film producer and in the 1980s served as the president of worldwide production at MGM/UA. Sidney and Joanna were close friends with Freddie and his wife, Corinna Tsopei. Fields died in 2007.

With the carriage of a gentleman, he passed through this world and left his mark. To those of us who knew him, his name was Freddie Fields, a wearer of many hats—friend, husband, father, grandfather, great-grandfather. An adventurer, a romantic, a courageous taker of risks in all things creative, a connoisseur of culture and art. A gentleman who was unafraid to speak his mind, stand his ground, or captain his own ship through the unforgiving storms of life, whenever the need arose.

Before we actually met, I had heard of Freddie Fields through the exploits of his many talents—in the entertainment industry at large and motion pictures in particular, back in the days when our bones were young and strong. But we were not destined to meet until we each had centered our ambitions on the professional world of the American motion picture industry, more than fifty years ago. Since then, we have lived to see ourselves through difficult times, and through magnificent times, when our bones were young and strong.

We have worked together with satisfying results, each in our own way, and—when our bones began to grow brittle—we were obliged to acknowledge the process with grace. I was a witness to his having done exactly that over these recent years. And I can truly say, no debt owed, no promises remain unfulfilled between his life and mine. As friends, we have each thanked the other for that.

The last time we sat at dinner, he was surrounded by family and friends, smiling, regaling others with his quiet humor and his subtle wit. That evening, Freddie was the Freddie I have always known. I was moved and couldn't help but admire not only his courage

Fields and director John Huston on the set of *Victory* (1981), one of a dozen films Fields produced in the mid-1970s and '80s.

but also the authority he seemed to have exercised over the closing of his life.

To my mind, the world has become a better place because Freddie Fields has passed this way. The quality of the man will surely linger across generations of young, strong bones yet to come—some of whom will take the reins of the entertainment industry and its many facets and make it better yet, make it an expression of thanks to all the Freddie Fieldses who have helped shape the world of entertainment and American motion pictures into an indispensable part of our ongoing culture.

For some of us the world will be fractionally imbalanced for a little while. Then it will correct itself, as it always has. In the process—as always—family members, friends, acquaintances, and admirers will face the many difficult, but necessary, adjustments that inevitably arise when someone so loved, so respected, so admired goes away. But our restorative powers—like the world's—will kick in, and we will make the many difficult adjustments necessary to hold the life of the departed loved one in our embrace forever.

Rest in peace, Freddie. Be at ease, Corinna and family.

He will be remembered.

He will be remembered.

MARTIN RITT

Film director Martin Ritt made his feature debut with the 1957 film *Edge of the City*, in which Sidney starred as a supervisor and mentor to a white dockworker played by John Cassavetes. Ritt would later direct Sidney opposite Paul Newman, Joanne Woodward, and Diahann Carroll in the jazz-infused *Paris Blues* (1961). Blacklisted early in his career, Ritt often made films with an overt social message. He passed away in 1990.

The common knowledge, we all share. Actor, director, writer, horse player, group theatre participant, blacklisted target, et cetera. But beyond the common knowledge, there is a Martin Ritt who lives in the privacy of our thoughts. There he influences, he entertains, he teaches, he inspires, and for those of us who, like me, have housed that Marty Ritt in our inner lives for close to forty years, he was most of all a reminder. When lines were blurred because tough choices cloud our vision, his life was there to remind us that the right choice was no less right because it was painful. When integrity required we stand up and take the heat, he reminded us that we grow stronger when we simply stand up and take the heat. When friendships and loyalties needed attention

Sidney with costar Joanne Woodward on the set of Martin Ritt's *Paris Blues* (1961), in which he plays a jazz saxophonist opposite fellow expat musician Paul Newman. The final film was highly altered from its controversial first screenplay, which had featured interracial romance. OPPOSITE: Ritt and Carroll with Sidney, on location in Paris in November 1960.

and fidelity, Marty Ritt and Walter Bernstein would come to mind. Marty Ritt and Bob Radnitz would come to mind. We know, too, that courage and candor complement each other because we have seen them at work in the Martin Ritt each of us knows. We are all better for having known him, and we will all be better if the Martin we house in our inner selves continues to remind us how to do it. Between his family and his friends, the Marty Ritt each of us knows will be around to light the way of those he left behind.

SARAH VAUGHAN

Discovered at an amateur contest at Harlem's Apollo Theater in 1942, Sarah Vaughan was soon hired by bandleader Billy Eckstine before embarking on a successful solo career. The legendary contralto was described by Quincy Jones, with whom she recorded one of her signature tunes, "Misty," in 1957, as "the most musical singer America has ever known." Vaughan died in April 1990.

Prior to his death, African American Scholar W. E. B. Du Bois left this message to the world:

I am going to take a long, deep and endless sleep. This is not a punishment, but a privilege to which I have looked forward for years. I have loved my work, I have loved people and my play, but always I have been uplifted by the thought that what I have done well will live long and justify my life; that what I have done ill or never finished can now be handed on to others for endless days to be finished, perhaps better than I could have done. And that peace is my applause!

Our lives have been enriched by so many great performers, none greater than Sarah Vaughan. She was called "Sassy"—I call us lucky for having experienced the Sarah Vaughan phenomenon.

Sarah Vaughan . . . even to say her name is music. I first met Sarah many, many years ago in a small jazz club. I sat mesmerized. She had a golden voice. It touched the heart and calmed the spirit. And I, like so many others, became a fan. Frank Sinatra once said, "I wish I could sing like her." The woman was extraordinary.

She was, by any standard or definition, the complete singer. And although Sarah did sing some things better than others, she could, in fact, sing everything. Surely, the angels must be rejoicing now that they have Sarah in their choir.

If we live three lifetimes, there will never be another Sarah Vaughan. She is beyond category . . . beyond imitation.

OPPOSITE: Vaughan had only one role in a Hollywood film—as a nightclub singer in 1960's *Murder, Inc.*—but her recordings grace the soundtracks of dozens of movies and TV shows.

CHARLES ALLEN BLACKWELL

Charlie Blackwell was a dancer and stage manager for numerous Broadway productions, which is where Sidney met him in the late 1950s. He wrote the screenplay to *A Piece of the Action* (1977), a story that Sidney directed and co-starred in about con men who are coerced into mentoring unemployed youth at a Black community center. He also performed a rewrite on Sidney's buddy comedy *Stir Crazy* (1980) and later assisted on an autobiographical, one-person stage show for Sidney, which was ultimately not produced. Blackwell passed away in 1995.

There are moments, occurrences, circumstances, conditions in life that are and will forever remain outside human understanding. I cannot therefore explain, for instance, why Charlie was such a magical force. Why he seemed at times to be the father of the universe. Why we all felt safe and absolutely trusting in his presence. Why the world we saw through his eyes was better than otherwise and promised in time to be even more than that. Why was the environment of Charlie Blackwell such a restful place for more than the body? Why had nature chosen him to be a symbol of the best in all of us? I cannot truly say. I cannot explain. But I can tell you what I believe.

I believe there were purposes to Charlie's life that included us all present here today—and more. I believe he will live on in things we say and do, in ways we treat each other. And the extent to which we open ourselves to the joys of life in these years we have left in each other's company. Just as he was a shining example for a better world, a better world would be the monument we all could have a hand in structuring to the life of Charlie Blackwell.

I loved him dearly and will miss him forever and will try not to be too resentful that he left us so early. Because I must, with respect, assume that nature had need of him someplace else. So, while we have grounds to complain, let us also be thankful that he came our way and has left his light behind.

To Frances, David, Lisa, and the rest of the family, we, his friends, stand with you and share your loss in this time of sorrow. And I also believe, through him and Frances, I have come to understand the deepest, purest meaning of integrity. In that family, integrity is more than a word. It is more than an element independently floating high above us, waiting for someone or something to elevate itself within range of its touch. In that family it is not a condition called into existence by words imaginatively arranged; it is not a compliment, nor a distinction ceremoniously bestowed by the state. In that family it is an accompaniment. It never comes out of thin air; it always travels in close company with other forces. It is almost always found side by side with character or shoulder to shoulder with decency. Step by step it moves alongside fidelity, honesty, selflessness, and compassion. It is always there to heal when dignity is stripped from human life and trampled on with calculated disregard.

I also believe that in troubled times when words fail to light our way, primal memory sends instinct to guide us in the dark and lead us towards the light.

I also believe that in troubled times when words fail to light our way, primal memory sends instinct to guide us in the dark and lead us towards the light. I also believe that in troubled times when spoken words lose their power, the language of the heart still speaks, and the language of the soul responds. There-fore, we can speak in silence, feel each other's pain, and share the loss.

Still, to all of us, Charlie's friends, I offer this gentle reminder. When missing him becomes unbearable, we need only look into our hearts and there he'll be. When we need to hear his voice, we need only to be silent. Of course, we all know that. But it will take a bit of an effort to understand that he will be everywhere at once.

In all our hearts, in our thoughts, in the infinite reaches of the cosmos itself. From infinity inward, to the edge of the known universe, the presence of his values will be felt. From there, again inward across one hundred billion galaxies, his existence and his humanity will be duly noted by and included into that vast consciousness that encompasses the oneness of everything. Inward still into our own galaxy with its one hundred billion stars, one of which sits off in a lonely section of a spiral arm with nine planets swirling in attendance. Nowhere, in the limitlessness of the cosmos, will there be an atom unaware of the wonders we know as Charlie Blackwell. Back here on this small place, swirling in attendance to our sun sitting ninety-three million miles away, his work is done. And well done. A delicate, fragile, miraculous entity—precious and priceless, rare and unique—has touched us all, and we will surely be the better for it and so will the family of man.

DANIEL PETRIE

The director of the film adaptation of *A Raisin in the Sun* (1961), in which Sidney reprised the role he originated on Broadway, as well as the respected crime film *Fort Apache, the Bronx* (1981), Daniel Petrie got his start on television and later won a pair of Emmys for his work in two popular miniseries on the Roosevelts. Petrie later served on the faculty of the American Film Institute. He maintained a long friendship with Sidney until his death in 2004.

After all the affection for—and appreciation of—the creative wonders of Daniel's full and memorable artistic life, one would think there's nothing left to say. Not true. We could, in fact, be here into the evening. I for one—the truth be told—could take us clearly past midnight. But firm reins in responsible hands have demanded that we not wander beyond the path of brevity. Still, it would obviously take more time than that for you to really know the true depth at which Daniel Petrie has been held in my esteem these past forty-odd years.

With that said, here we are again with further expressions of love in varying forms. For this husband, this father, this grandfather, this friend, this fellow artist.

While most men are different in appearance, only a few are different at the core. And fewer still are different in ways that cannot be explained. Chosen by some mysterious process we are not meant to unravel, these precious few will live out their lives in long, lonely journeys straight toward the hearts and minds of their fellow human beings, and there reveal to us the selves we cannot see . . . the worlds we never knew existed . . . show us how wonder and magic awaken inside us when the energy of new ideas ignites our imagination and pulls at our curiosity.

His mark will forever be visible in his unique cinematic portraits of the complexities of the human heart—and will stand always as rock-solid testament to his creative imagination.

OPPOSITE: **Sidney with Diana Sands and Ruby Dee in** *A Raisin in the Sun*

Claudia McNeil as Lena Younger and Sidney as her son Walter Lee in *A Raisin in the Sun*.

Such journeys were destined to be the stuff from which the life's work of Daniel Petrie would be fashioned. His mark will forever be visible in his unique cinematic portraits of the complexities of the human heart—and will stand always as rock-solid testament to his creative imagination.

I knew Dan was special from the first directorial instructions he gave me. I soon discovered that in his choreography, actors moved from point A to point B simply because it would have been unnatural for them not to. The words his actors spoke came from an internal place. They were an extension of a need to reveal, or obscure, or deny, or give of something inside themselves—something that needed to be addressed.

When a seamlessness was required for the effectiveness of a scene, he conspired with actors in a private way. I know—I was there at some such times, like others in this room. Working with him was a joy in the extreme. The things I learned of value from that Daniel Petrie we all knew I have tried to carry over to every subsequent job I have done.

So, Daniel—this afternoon is merely a thumb sketch, a smidgen of what all of us gathered here have to say. But we must reluctantly save the rest for another time. You know how Dorothea is when she cracks the whip—she cracks the whip—three minutes—and not a second more. And since I know who the boss is in your family, I'm certainly not going to chance the cracking of the whip.

Instead, here, Daniel, in the wisest use of my remaining time, let me share with you, your family and friends, some of the thoughts I've had on the element of genius. How do we spot it, in a great surgeon, a great painter, a great filmmaker? Is it bigger than a breadbasket? Or is it not as large as a grain of sand? Or is it as tiny as a subatomic particle? Indeed, does genius have a shape or form? If we cannot spot it by size or shape, then how do we know we're in its presence? Because, I believe, it leaves a mark on the work of an individual surgeon, on the canvas of an individual painter, on the vision of an individual filmmaker. Through firsthand experience, I have been privileged to witness the element of genius in the work of Norman Jewison, Daniel Petrie, Richard Brooks, Sydney Pollack, and Guy Green. That element in their vision inspired actors to reach beyond their limits, led them to new, illuminating choices that clearly articulated the writer's intent. America's film industry would be considerably less vibrant without the element of genius captured in their work. You have seen it on the screen. Some of us have seen it in action—it is something to behold.

So, my friend, be at ease in your well-earned rest. And in the event we're all destined to collect together again—in another place for yet another first rehearsal—well then, we'll all be seeing you later.

HAVE KNOWN GEORGE STEVENS, JR.

OR A VERY LONG TIME. GEORGE AND I

HAVE WORKED TOGETHER, ON FILMS,

ND FOR THE CAUSES THAT WE BOTH

BELIEVE IN. AND, WHEN YOU WORK

WITH GEORGE STEVENS, ART AND

CTIVISM ARE NEVER VERY FAR APART.

GEORGE IS AN EXTRAORDINARY

ERSON. IF HE COMMITS TO

OMETHING, HE WILL GET IT DONE.

HE'S ABSOLUTELY FEARLESS.

A CALL FROM GEORGE.

ION. AND IT WAS VERY

HIM.

ON BECAME THE AMERICAN

ITUTE. I AM PROUD TO HAVE

S THE INAUGURAL VICE-

N OF THE BOARD OF A-F-I

DE GREGORY PECK.

NG YOU MAY NOT KNOW

EORGE IS, THAT HE IS ALSO

MELY GIFTED DIRECTOR.

E

E IN

Y HIS

RY EVER

IOW

T IS AN

S EQUAL

ND

UD T

R TO

DETROIT REMARKS
DINNER (2)
6/8/02

HAD I KNOWN THAT YOU GUYS
WERE HAVING SO MUCH FUN--
EVERY YEAR – FOR 39 YEARS—

I WOULD HAVE BEEN BEGGING FOR
AN INVITATION FROM 1961.

 WHAT YOU DO HERE FOR ART AND
CULTURE IS PHENOMENAL—

 AND SHOULD BE DUPLICATED IN
EVERY CITY IN AMERICA—

ART AND CULTURE SPEAKS MOST
CLEARLY—
AND MOST FORCEFULLY—

ABOUT THE INCREDIBLE JOURNEY
OF THE HUMAN SPIRIT—

NY OTHER ENDEAVOR THE
OF MAN HAS EVER
AKEN.

WONDERFUL EVENING
S—
T IN MIND OF A
STING EVENING OUT OF THE
ATION OF AN ANONYMOUS

ENING TOOK PLACE,
, THREE HUNDRED AND
OUSAND YEARS AGO—

DAWN OF HUMAN

MAN--WHO HAD …JUST
INSIDE A WARM CAVE …

RIMITIVE, THEIR
TIVE, THEIR ART

E WARMTH

STY

NGUE,

THE

ARE

E—

THEY

RE

ARTS & TRADITION

Through the arts we have come to
understand who we are and of
what we are capable.

Sidney's public addresses often touched on themes of creation, the human imagination, and the role of art in society. He often explored these concepts in speeches to arts organizations, including the Academy of Motion Picture Arts and Sciences and various museums and institutions of higher learning around the country.

His innate curiosity about the scientific world influenced the way he thought about his own work. He was intrigued by the cosmos, was friends with astrophysicist Carl Sagan, and even wrote a fiction book on the subject—*Montaro Caine* (2013). Again and again, he returned to the image of the single-cell organism crawling out of the mud as an allegory for the struggle of modern man to survive against the elements—both natural and institutional.

A major figure in the twentieth century's most celebrated art form—a prolific actor, writer, director, and film producer—Sidney knew that he was part of a meaningful cultural history and a powerful social force. His speeches to arts organizations therefore dwelled on themes of artistic courage, activism, integrity, tradition, and the human spirit, and they also spotlighted creative personalities that had an impact on Sidney and his career.

GEORGE STEVENS JR.

Honorary Oscar

Sidney presented his friend, producer George Stevens Jr., with an Honorary Oscar at the Academy of Motion Picture Arts and Sciences' Governors Awards ceremony in 2012. His brief intro spoke to Stevens's activism and his founding of the American Film Institute in the 1960s.

I have known George Stevens Jr. for a very long time. George and I have worked together on films and for the causes that we both believe in. And when you work with George Stevens, art and activism are never very far apart.

George is an extraordinary person. If he commits to something, he will get it done. He's absolutely fearless.

In 1967, I got a call from George. He had a vision. And it was very clear to him. That vision became the American Film Institute. I am proud to have served as the inaugural vice chairman of the board of AFI alongside Gregory Peck.

Something you may not know about George is that he is also an extremely gifted director. I had the unique privilege of being directed by both George in *Separate but Equal* and by his father in *The Greatest Story Ever Told*. When I worked with him, I immediately

"To be handed an Academy Award by Sidney—with his stature and humanity—was the crowning touch," wrote Stevens of the event.

understood how George feels about film. It is an art. And actors are artists equal to the great painters and composers.

On behalf of the Academy and actors everywhere, I am proud to present this Honorary Oscar to George Stevens Jr.

THE DETROIT INSTITUTE OF ARTS
BAL AFRICAIN GALA

For several years, the Detroit Institute of Arts hosted its annual "Bal Africain" fundraising gala to benefit its African art collection and associated programs. In June 2002, Sidney was invited to speak at that year's event. His remarks touched on the origins of art and the human spirit that kindled those initial creative sparks.

Had I known that you guys were having so much fun, every year for thirty-nine years, I would have been begging for an invitation from 1961. What you do here for art and culture is phenomenal and should be duplicated in every city in America.

> *Art and culture speak most clearly and most forcefully about the incredible journey of the human spirit than any other endeavor the family of man has ever undertaken.*

Art and culture speak most clearly and most forcefully about the incredible journey of the human spirit than any other endeavor the family of man has ever undertaken.

As this wonderful evening unfolds, I am put in mind of a contrasting evening out of the imagination of an anonymous writer. That evening took place perhaps 360,000 years ago at the dawn of human history, when a man—who had just stepped inside a warm cave to escape the chill of a frosty night—said in an unknown tongue, to whomever was present around a fire, "Good evening, ladies and gentlemen. Please excuse the intrusion. My name is Ug. I'm a hunter. My wife and two children are outside in the cold. They are gatherers. We wonder if we can join you just until the sun comes up in the morning, and we'll be off." They were allowed the warmth of the cave and a place near the fire. When the morning came, they thanked the dwellers of the cave and continued on their way.

Imagine what it must have been like back then in that cave, around that fire. A collection of early humans, the symbolic forebearers, as it were, of the entire human family. Themselves primitive, their culture primitive—their art, likewise, primitive. Yet through instinct and intuition they had come to regard culture and art as among the necessities for survival, and left their presence and their history etched on the walls of caves to symbolize their existence. Messages, in effect, of how they lived and died—even as they sat huddled around that fire with a more immediate objective in mind: to stay warm and safe from harm until the morning came. Then, exiting the sanctuary of that cave with a different objective—to stay alive through another day of hunting and gathering the daily essentials of life, from the harsh and dangerous environment of those earliest of years, surviving brutal encounters with hunters from enemy tribes, searching for the same food, surviving predator animals roaming the landscape, hunting for opportunities to kill and eat anything—man or beast—careless enough to be caught off their guard for a fraction of a second.

Three hundred sixty thousand years later, here we are on this glorious evening because those original forefathers and original foremothers to us all endured. They persevered. They transformed themselves through thousands of generations over hundreds of thousands of years, by a constant effort at trying to reach beyond their limitations, learning about life and art through trial and error, painting on the walls of caves, sculpting with stone tools, dancing after smoking some unknown weed, drinking some five-hundred-proof fermented grain that made some of them think they were birds, [that they] could fly. Send others sneaking off to do the nasty-nasty in the back of a cave. Don't get the wrong impression—they were having as much fun then as we're having now. Maybe more! They didn't have to go to no gym to stay in shape. Surviving from morning to night was Viagra enough for some of those guys. If you add to that some of that unknown weed and throw in some five-hundred-proof fermented grains— Hey! Is there any wonder why planet Earth is having an overpopulation problem? There you have it.

All of which is to say they and we are all made of the same stuff—weaknesses and strengths, hopes and dreams, and a need to leave evidence of our existence etched on the walls of our time. For them and for us, art and culture will speak the loudest and the longest of our moment in the sun. Assuming it is correct that our existence reaches back to that time, that cave, and those occupants, I would like to think that more than a little of the best of them is still running in the veins of all of us here tonight.

My thanks again to the Bal Africain for a fabulous experience in a wonderful city. And I, indeed, look forward to returning.

STANLEY KRAMER

Stanley Kramer was a director, writer, and producer of several landmark films of the mid-twentieth century—among them, *The Defiant Ones* (1958) and *Guess Who's Coming to Dinner* (1967), in which Sidney played starring roles. Kramer's films were mainstream entertainments that pointedly addressed societal problems—a recipe for box office success, if not unanimous critical appreciation. Nevertheless, his impact on Sidney's career was critical and inarguable; the director is largely responsible for crafting the screen persona we know today.

After Kramer passed away in 2001, Sidney spoke publicly about the director on several occasions. What follows is a selection of his words touching upon Kramer's influence as well as the importance of pursuing truth with courage in one's art and life.

I know, as a fact, that the courage of this man has made a better man of me.

I have known men who—if their measure were taken—would be found to be living out their lives in ways peculiar to their nature, men who have tamed their natural instincts to meet the required standards for indifference. Men who have a position of no position on too many of the issues that—if left unaddressed—will corrode further the dignity and integrity of human life. I know men who will not take responsibility for a choice—even a correct one—if a modest cost to ego and self-perception is attached. Men who, in the words of the hippie, "can make the talk but can't walk the walk." Men who need an audience to witness their giving, but exercise the right to privacy in their taking. These men I have known, because more than once in my life, I too have been at some of these stations myself. But I know a man who, again in the words of the hippie, "made his moves and paid his dues" as he walked the walk on through his life—to victory sometimes, to defeat sometimes, but always accepting responsibility for the choices that took him to either place. I know a man whose biographical material and credits need not be restated here, unless one chooses to impress with the awesome stature of the artist they suggest. Still, it must be said that this man I know has not been properly thanked by his fellows in direct proportion to the debt owed.

Sidney's first project with producer-director Stanley Kramer was *The Defiant Ones* (1958), a racial drama in which he played an escaped prisoner shackled to costar Tony Curtis.

I welcome this opportunity to honor the life of a great friend and filmmaker. It was a profound experience for me to have had the privilege to work under the direction of such a remarkable talent. It allowed me the great opportunity to work with Spencer Tracy, Katharine Hepburn, Tony Curtis, and many, many others. It was a fabulous experience

that galvanized, for me, a career I had never dreamed possible. *The Defiant Ones*, *Pressure Point*, and *Guess Who's Coming to Dinner* were films that pushed the limits of the status quo and changed the game of the film industry—not to mention the world—considerably.

Stanley Kramer was quite a remarkable human being. He was an unusual person in so many ways, especially in regard to the motion picture industry. In the many years I knew him, I will never forget the extraordinary gifts that personified the essence of Stanley Kramer—film director, film producer, visionary, family man, friend—all of which added up to his life having become a remarkable example of what the American film industry has made of itself: a competitor worldwide.

These were experiences that had a profound impact on me as a young actor in a film industry that was not inclined, in those days, to hire or embrace young African American actors. It took a certain kind of person to have had the insight and courage to bring to the forefront social issues that were difficult to address, and commonly ignored, by the general public. Many of Stanley's films did just that, and although he was not the only one, he was one of the first among a considerable body of extraordinary filmmakers much like himself—like Joe Mankiewicz, like George Stevens, like James Clavell—all of whom were of the Stanley Kramer texture.

I was fortunate enough to have been chosen by each of them, and I stand here in true appreciation of the Stanley Kramer I knew. His craftsmanship continues to raise the bar higher and higher yet—to levels that will forever enrich the future and art of filmmaking and filmmakers worldwide.

The Hollywood of Stanley Kramer's youth was not a courageous place. Nor was it a hospitable place for someone like myself—perceived as different enough to be viewed as a trespasser, prowling too close to the edges of some private domain, near which he did not belong. The Hollywood of Stanley Kramer's youth and mine contained striking similarities. At roughly the same time, we were both on the margins of the American social reality, for vastly different reasons. He was coming with ideas ahead of the times, and I was coming without credentials—a trespasser hoping to plead his case. Each heading in different directions, on different missions. Still, for reasons unknown, our paths were fated to cross. I would eventually be privileged to accompany him from time to time on short stretches of his journey, long enough to witness the moment-to-moment transformation his purpose would bring to bear on the Hollywood we knew. It seems to me that courage of a special kind came to visit on the heels of his arrival here.

And while it stayed and roamed the town in low profile for years on end, it often was reminded to be careful where it stepped. And be watchful of its tongue.

Such image as courage now has in the Hollywood of today is owed in no small measure to the handful of men like Stanley Kramer,

who stood fast on difficult days and aligned themselves four-square with the values by which they conducted their lives—as men, as husbands, as fathers, as citizens, and as artists. Men who came to town with expectations, men who arrived fully ready to accept as a given that they would have to swim against the tide sometimes.

The life's work of Stanley Kramer is a testament to courage, to integrity, to honesty, and to determination. Had he not elected to swim against the tide when the currents were sometimes at their strongest, we would not

Sidney on the set of *Guess Who's Coming to Dinner* with director Stanley Kramer and actors Spencer Tracy and Katharine Hepburn. His last film role, Tracy died just seventeen days after filming ended.

have had the opportunity to experience the cinematic impact of such thought-provoking, revolutionary ideas that stood at the heart of his unique film career.

For forty-three years he was a true friend, and in my views and feelings he will forever remain a fearless, courageous maker of films, a man among men.

THE DALLAS CENTER FOR THE PERFORMING ARTS FOUNDATION

The AT&T Performing Arts Center in Dallas, Texas, opened in 2009 after a multiyear fund-raising campaign and construction phase. Seven years earlier, Sidney had appeared at a gala event to help raise money for the facilities and returned in April 2004 to speak to the arts organization. He was, along with Julie Andrews, Tommy Lee Jones, and Hilary Swank, one of several notable celebrities who lent their support to the project. Sidney took the opportunity to speak about ambition, the importance of struggle, and the evolution of self-expression.

Life, as best we can tell, began by chance or design as a one-celled amoeba in a cauldron of boiling chemicals, otherwise known as the primordial soup. That's as close as the tools of science have been able to place us to that monumental moment: the birth of life.

How, one might wonder, could a one-celled amoeba—without a brain, frenetically squiggling about in its steamy environment—happen, somehow, to assess its circumstances and, somehow, decide on a survival strategy, and then, somehow, struggle to point itself towards a better life? A one-celled amoeba without a brain? Hard to imagine!

I, for one, haven't the faintest idea how it could have done that. But that is exactly what it did. Had it not done so, we wouldn't be gathered here tonight as indisputable manifestations of its evolutionary struggle to survive. What mysterious force, or sense, or instinct, or impulse could have been driving that amoeba? Destiny? Perhaps. Or could it have been ambition to become a two-celled amoeba? To that end, survival had to have been fought for and won, in order that a generation of two-celled amoebas would one day set their sights on a three-celled existence.

And so on and so on, over the billions of years it took for the primordial soup to cool, for the oceans to form, for the continents to emerge, and for gravity to figure out how to pull moisture up from the oceans into the atmosphere and send it back to the continents in the form of freshwater rain and snow. By chance or design, oceans, continents, gravity, lightning that struck the earth and thunder that rolled overhead created opportune conditions for ambition-driven amoebas to transform themselves over billions of generations into a wondrous variety of living creatures, species after species appearing in profusion, one more complex than the other in design and durability, in size and shape, in texture and color, adaptability and vulnerability. Each unique unto itself.

Now here we are, all because that one-celled amoeba—the first tiny spark of life—was ambitious enough, tough enough, courageous enough to struggle enough, to wrestle the future of life out of a hostile environment. That spark of life would, in time, create a hostile environment of its own, wherein the most basic of nature's laws must always rule supreme. That, apparently, was how she wanted it! That was how she intended it to be. A hostile environment, in which predator and prey are both obliged to live and die by the same principle: survival by any means available. No quarter asked; none given. That—it appears—was the fundamental rule of the game of life for billions of years after the one-celled amoeba and before the earliest members of the human family were to make their appearance on the stage of living things. We were new. We were neither the swiftest not the strongest of nature's crea-

tures. We were vulnerable. Our defenses were inadequate on the ground and in the trees. At the bottom line, long ago, nature had made her point unmistakably clear. To the predator, she said: You kill, you eat. To the prey she said: You escape, you live. She let it be known that survival will never be a slam dunk for any species. For us—the new arrivals—instinct and impulse had to carry the weight of our survival. They were all we could muster to defend against the swiftest and the strongest of all the creatures of the earth.

Out of the one-celled amoeba and its inherent ambitions have flowed an evolutionary history of such awesome complexity that the tools of science bow respectfully in the presence of all that remains yet to be learned.

And for us—you and I, the family of man, the human species—since we are both predator and prey at alternate times, survival, indeed, has never been a slam dunk. Our defenses, instincts, and impulses were frequently overwhelmed by the swift and the strong. But we have survived. Tonight, we are here to bow symbolically to instincts, impulses, and one of their most effective tools: art. Together, they have been largely responsible for engineering our species' survival through times of unspeakable peril, across journeys that tested our will and challenged our resolve, through battles we have lost to the strong and the swift. Wherever surviving members of the human family are still walking the earth, instinct, impulse, and art are their constant companions.

The arts that will nurture you and your children in the Dallas Center for the Performing Arts are an inheritance sent down across the bloodline from ancestors, long gone, to remind us of who they were and how they came to be. To remind us that our instincts and impulses are functions of a primal memory that link them and us across millions of years.

In time, some of early mankind would be driven by instinct and impulse along a parallel path, seeking the tools of self-expression, which would lead those artistically inclined to paint on the walls of caves, to design, choreograph, and create ritual dances to the sounds of primitive drums.

How did we, the family of man, come upon those artistic expressions? By chance? I think not. The need to know and understand who we were and why compelled the search for answers. But first, answers required language—the process of thought, the awareness of consciousness—and thousands of years of trial-and-error experiences—experiences that affect our choices at given times, our mood at others, make us laugh and move us to tears, touch our hearts and cradle our minds, lull us to sleep, bolster our courage, and applaud our bravery. Life without trial-and-error experience would be the lesser for it. Because the struggle for survival was intense, immediate,

unforgiving, excruciatingly painful, and at times unbearable, we are constantly reminded of our imperfections. But because we are imperfect doesn't mean we shouldn't try to reverse that state of being. Free will, in the human personality, is known to have leveled a surprising number of rebellious playing fields. But a word of caution! Imagine what it would have been like if we came in perfect—already grown, already knowing everything, perfectly well adjusted, perfectly handsome, perfectly beautiful, unshakably confident in ourselves, automatic bank accounts. Plus, aging ever so slowly at a rate dictated by our egos—or not aging at all. Sounds great. But the downside will be costly. We would have missed the joy of having a childhood, the wonder of daydreams designed by a child's imagination, the comfort of loving, parental arms when we're frightened by thunder's roar and lightning's flash, or the dark, or our first day at school, or our

Embellishing, shaping, inspiring, supporting, influencing, challenging it, daring it to explore, to stretch, to broaden, to deepen—and by so doing, enlightening the self.

first friend. We would know nothing of the multitude of random experiences, good and bad, that one by one, day by day, year by year, sketch a real-life portrait of the struggles an unpredictable life must endure as it moves towards its own destiny. Only in such a life are art, music, dance, language, theatre, literature, opera, songs of life and death constant chords in the rhythms of that life. Embellishing, shaping, inspiring, supporting, influencing, challenging it, daring it to explore, to stretch, to broaden, to deepen—and by so doing, enlightening the self. In the perfect person, there would be no need or room for the above, leaving him or her with the prospect of boredom as a constant companion. But thanks to the infinite wisdom of God for making us the perfectly imperfect creatures that we are. Because we are imperfect, we seek, we explore, we refine, sometimes we stretch ourselves beyond our limits, reaching for something. Something that leaves us in the estimate of ourselves, standing high as good and worthy human beings whose fondest wish and greatest hope is for the world at large and most especially family, friends, acquaintances, and our bosses to concur. Then that certainly would be a cool, cool thing and the world would certainly be a cool, cool place. Through the arts we have come to understand who we are and of what we are capable.

The performing arts enable us to portray life as it might be and to appreciate it as it is. In describing theatre, Thornton Wilder once said, "We live in what is, but we find a thousand ways not to face it. Great theater strengthens our faculty to face it." From Sophocles's *Oedipus the King* and Shakespeare's *Hamlet*, through Tennessee Williams's *A Streetcar Named Desire*, we walk in the shadows of the actors amidst the characters of real life and, in so doing, we come to understand the humanity in ourselves. George Farquhar once said:

> *Like hungry guests, a sitting audience looks.*
> *Plays are like suppers; poets are the cooks.*
> *The founder's you; the table is this place.*
> *The carvers we; the prologue is the grace.*
> *Each act a course, each scene a different dish.*

If you are students of history you understand that among the most impactful achievements in the history of civilization were, in a very real sense, journeys traveled by remarkable people with a capacity to imagine. Performances in this place will stir your emotions, stimulate your imaginations, and immerse you into the creative process.

The point is that art is essential. Its effect is on character. It avails nothing unless it ennobles and strengthens that. Its use is for life. Its aim is not beauty but goodness. In reaching for that, we honor the hard-earned gifts of instincts and impulses, sent down to us through "primal memory dot com" from ancestors long gone who wanted us to know who they were and what they had made of life.

BUCKLEY SCHOOL FUNDRAISER – 11-20-04

R JOANNA AND I THE REFLECTION OF THE BUCKLEY SCHOOOL

SEEN THROUGH THE LIVES OF OUR CHILDREN ARE AMONG

R MOST TREASURED MEMORIES. THERE THEY WERE, LITTLE

OPLE LEAVING HOME IN THE MORNING, RETURNING IN THE

TERNOON KNOWING A LITTLE MORE THAN THEY DID *the day* BEFORE

OUT THE BIG WIDE WORLD IN WHICH THEY LIVED. A WORLD

LED WITH MYSTERY AND WONDER AND SO MUCH MORE THAT
and

EY COULD NOT YET UNDERSTAND. BUT, DAY IN/DAY OUT, AT

E BUCKLEY SCHOOL, DISCOVERIES OF ONE KIND OR ANOTHER

ULD LIGHT UP THEIR INOCENT FACES WHILE QUIETLY

PTURING THEIR STILL VERY YOUNG IMAGINATIONS. SOME

COVERIES BOLSTERED THEIR SELF CONFIDENCE. OTHERS

ED SMALL THREATS THAT LOOMED LARGER THAN THE LEVEL

THEIR UNDERSTANDING COULD RECOGNIZE AND DISMISS.

USC GRADUATION ADDRESS 2000

Good EVENING ALL! HERE IS THE OUTSET

~~CLASS OF 2000~~, I AM PRESSED BY CONSCIENCE TO

ADMIT- THAT WHEN I FIRST RECEIVED YOUR MOST

GENEROUS INVITATION TO COME AND SPEAK, I WAS

TROUBLED BY THE THOUGHT OF WHAT COULD I POSSIBLY

HAVE OF INTREST TO SAY TO AN EDUCATED, WELL

ROUNDED, YOUNG, AWSOMELY COOL, *AUDIENCE* CLASS LIKE YOU.

I'VE NOT BEEN, TO MY SATISFACTION, <u>FULLY ABLE</u>

TO PUT THAT THOUGHT TO REST. IN FACT, WHILE WAITIN

TO BE INTRODUCED A FEW MINUTES AGO-THE GROUNDS

FOR MY EARLIER CONCERN INTENSIFIED-AS IT

GRADUALLY BECAME CLEAR THAT YOUR PRESENCE HERE

INDEED, SPEAKS OF QUICK MINDS, KEEN INTEREST,

VIBRANT CURIOSITIES AND EXPECTATIONS THAT

<u>THREATEN</u> TO KEEP ME ON MY TOES AND MAKE ME REACH

BEYOND MY GRASP.

RSTANDING.

THE PASSAGE OF TIME, JOANNA AND I HAVE W

VOLUTION OF OUR TWO LITTLE PEOPLE INTO FU

T HUMAN BEINGS. WHO HAVE DISCOVERED, TO

TS DELIGHT, THAT VALUES LEARNED AT A PLAC

EY ARE NOW A PART OF THEIR LIFE'S FOUNDAT

S, THEY STAND ON PRINCIPALS THAT ARTICUL

ARE. THEY HAVE REACHED THAT FINAL STAGE

E AND ACCEPT THE DEEPER UNDERSTANDING

ICTIONS FIRMLY HELD, WILL, SOMEWHERE ALON

TEST ONE'S STRENGTH OF CHARACTER.

ONE'S SHOULD EXPECT, THEREFORE, TO SWIM A

DE SOMETIMES. THAT THEY SHOULD EXPECT, I

STY, FAIRNESS, DIGNITY AND COMPASSION TO

NCE IN ALL OF THEIR UNDERTAKINGS.

St. Marks Graduation Speech
2002

GOOD ~~AFTERNOON~~ *MORNING* EVERYONE…

CLASS OF 2002

<u>I</u> <u>AM</u> <u>DELIGHTED</u> <u>TO</u> <u>BE</u> <u>HERE</u>.

That sentence is,

~~THERE IS~~ --A COMMENT--

~~A SENTENCE~~

A REMARK—

AN EXPRESSION THAT MIGHT

TRIGGER A QUESTION IN YOUR

MIND--

<u>WHY</u> IS THIS <u>GRANDFATHERLY</u>

LOOKING GUY—

<u>SO</u> DELIGHTED TO BE HERE?

IS HE <u>REALLY</u> --<u>REALLY</u> DELIGHTED

TO BE HERE—

OR IS HE JUST SAYING THAT? –

AND IF HE <u>IS</u> JUST SAYING THAT –

FOR SAYING

ATIVE

CHER ASK

Such A Thought.

--A PARENT

T WHO IS A

MINE AND A

THE SCHOOL.

ELIGHTED TO

D TO BE

LOOKING
—

THE NEXT
GENERATION

*If restless expectations are thrashing
about inside you in anticipation of what the
future holds, that's a good sign.*

E ver the inspiring figure—a man who represented so much for
so many and signaled a shifting cultural landscape through
his defining movie roles—Sidney was often invited to give
commencement addresses to graduates of universities and second-
ary schools. His life story itself was inspirational, and the experiences
he lived through were valuable instruction to those about to step out
on their own. A self-taught man who highly valued education, Sidney
enjoyed passing down the wisdom he had accumulated through years of
struggle and hard-won success.

He spoke to graduates not only about pursuing their dreams, but
about the importance of having to struggle to attain those dreams, and
the knowledge and support that is passed down between generations
to help us reach our goals. In a few instances, he spoke to graduating
classes that included his favorite and most adoring audience members:
his own daughters.

Smart enough to recognize when he had something worth repeat-
ing, Sidney tended to reuse portions of earlier speeches, from borrowing
simple turns of phrase and restating themes to lifting whole passages
from one speech and placing them into another. Each instance of repetition was done with purpose and tailored to a specific audience, and
this practice speaks not just to Sidney's efficiency but also to his clarity
of vision. He knew exactly what he wanted to say.

100 BLACK MEN OF AMERICA

June 11, 1993
Fort Lauderdale, Florida

Sidney's daughter Pamela delivered this message from her father to the civic and mentoring organization 100 Black Men of America, which had been started thirty years earlier in New York City by leaders like baseball legend Jackie Robinson, physician William H. Hayling, sociologist and civil rights activist Cyril deGrasse Tyson, businessman J. Bruce Llewellyn, and eventual New York mayor David Dinkins. With chapters nationwide, "the 100" services disadvantaged and youth of color through community programs, educational development, leadership training, wellness initiatives, and more.

Its motto, "What They See Is What They'll Be," is the sort of wise aphorism that also applies to Sidney and other Black role models in the entertainment industry. Though brief, his statement to the group clearly shows his admiration for its mission to raise up the next generation—a theme in many of Sidney's public speeches.

Ladies and gentlemen, rooms like this are not new to us. We have been here before—dozens of times. We have drawn lines in the sand in rooms like this against diseases, against poverty, for education, for the elderly, for the young, for responsible government, for the underprivileged. We have given from our hearts, from our pockets, and of ourselves in rooms like these, and still we come—100 Black Men. We gather here, yet another time, in this familiar room where more money has been raised for good and worthy purposes than any other room in our collective experiences as 100 Black Men.

Most of us are not pop stars. Most of us are not household names. But all of us who have come to register our continued support for good and worthy purposes have also, by our presence here, articulated the strong sense of responsibility that characterizes us in this, the community of our roots.

It is for me an honor of distinction to simply be counted as one among the 100 Black Men, the most consistent organization that converts good and worthy purposes into concrete results. Thank you.

NEW YORK UNIVERSITY COMMENCEMENT

Sidney was invited to speak at NYU's 163rd commencement ceremonies in May 1995. He received an honorary doctor of fine arts degree, a moment that was made even more special by the presence of his daughter Sydney in the graduating class. Here he recounts part of his own life story, including his young adulthood in New York—where he learned to read, cut his teeth on the stage, and began to develop into the actor who would entertain generations. His description of the opening night of *Lysistrata* in 1946 was later used verbatim in his 2000 autobiography, *The Measure of a Man*.

I was born on February 20, 1927, unaware of everything that had happened on this planet, in this solar system, in this galaxy, in this universe before I arrived. It was to take a lifetime of inquiry, wonder, trial and error, and wide-eyed curiosity to fix myself in time and mark my brief presence in the onward journey of human history. A lifetime of trying to find out what the hell was going on before I got here has exercised my less-than-modest capabilities to the max.

Had I but known that four years at New York University would have armed me with information of such an enlightened sort, I wouldn't have spent seventy-four years laboriously accumulating what I now know. At the age of twenty-one, I would have known damn near everything I know today. At twenty-five, not only would I have known the how and the when of the beginning of the journey of human history, I might have even divined the purpose of the journey. Moreover, I would have known where to search, from time to time, for progress reports, and how to find the variety of scenarios which hint at the journey's possible destination. Clearly, with such

> *It was to take a lifetime of inquiry, wonder, trial and error, and wide-eyed curiosity to fix myself in time and mark my brief presence in the onward journey of human history.*

knowledge aforethought, I know I would have been able to fix myself in time at an earlier age and possibly have found a more meaningful role in the journey of human history. Under such circumstances, I would have been an alumnus of the class of '50. But that was not to be the way I would eventually accumulate the minimal amount of understanding I now might have. I was a slow kid. Life was my university. Trial and error were my teachers.

My daughter, on the other hand, was smiled upon from above. With four years of the university of New York City under her belt, she even knows about the beginning of the beginning—the big bang something or other. She knows that billions of years of preparation were necessary before the journey of human history could begin. She understood early in life that one learns, one absorbs, one discovers, or one perishes without ever knowing where one is in time. That my daughter is on the journey armed with enough information to possibly think of a role in which she might influence the course of human history in some small, useful way pleases me. I owe the university of New York City for my daughter's education. I owe the streets of New York City for mine—and the streets of Miami, Florida, and the streets of Nassau, and Cat Island in the Bahamas. Those are the kinds of places where I was taught that honor comes with responsibility. Where one pays as one goes. Where an unpredictable

mix of curiosity, risks, and rewards—unto themselves—can very often determine survival. It was on such a street that I first heard the words that would set my course and keep me steady at the wheel. On that morning in the summer of 1945, I had no way of knowing that trial and error, curiosity, risks, and rewards were positioned for a life-altering impact on my existence. Let's pick it up a half hour before the moment arrived.

I was a dishwasher. That's how I survived my early years in NYC. Minimal skills were required. Dishwashing provided a salary and three meals per day. I was in between job assignments on the morning in question, and my pockets were nearly empty. So empty, in fact, that if no dishwashing position was available, I was ready to glom on to any kind of work that a Black kid with no education might qualify for. I purchased a copy of the *Amsterdam News*, one of Harlem's leading newspapers, and started scanning the want-ad page for dishwasher openings.

The last page of want-ad boxes faced the theatrical page, which contained an article with a heading that read "actors wanted." The gist of which was that a theatre group called the American Negro Theatre was in need of actors for its next production. My mind got to spinning. My eyes bounced back and forth between the want-ad page and the theatrical page. "What the hell," I thought. "I've tried dishwashers wanted, porters wanted, janitors

Sidney was one of several honorary degree recipients at the 1995 NYU ceremony, including singer-songwriter Neil Diamond and historian Henry Louis Gates Jr.

wanted. Why not try actors wanted?" I figured I could do that. It didn't sound any more difficult than washing dishes or parking cars. And they didn't say they required any particular kind of training. But when I went in and was auditioned on the spot, the man in charge quickly let me know, and in no uncertain terms, that I was misguided in my assumptions. I had no training in acting. I could barely read! And to top it off I had a thick, singsong Bahamian accent. He snatched the script from my hands, spun me around, grabbed me by the scruff of my neck and the back of my pants, and marched me on my tippy-toes towards the door. He was seething, "You just get out of here and stop wasting people's time. Go get a job you could handle," he barked. "Get yourself a job as a dishwasher or something." That was the line he ended with as he threw me out and slammed the door.

I have to tell you, his comments stung worse than any wasp on any sapodilla tree back in my childhood. I hadn't mentioned to him that I was a dishwasher. How did he know? If he didn't know, then what was it about me that seemed to have implied to this stranger that a dishwasher's profession would accurately sum up my whole life's worth?

Whatever it was, I knew I had to change it or life was going to be mighty grim. And so, I set out on a course of self-improvement. I worked nights, and on my evening lunch breaks I sat in a quiet area of the restaurant where I was employed—near the entrance to the kitchen—reading the newspapers, trying to sound out each syllable of each unfamiliar word. An old Jewish waiter, noticing my efforts, took pity and offered to help. He became my tutor as well as my guardian angel of the moment. Each night we sat in the same booth in that quiet area of the restaurant, and he helped me learn to read better than I was able to before.

My immediate objective was to prove that I could be an actor. Not that I had any real desire to go on the stage, not that I had ever given it a thought. I simply needed to prove to that stranger that Sidney Poitier had a hell of a lot more to him than washing dishes. And it worked. The second time around they let me in.

But it was still no slam dunk. In fact, I made the cut only because there were so few guys and they needed some male bodies to round out the incoming class of new students. But not even that could keep me for long, given my lack of education and experience. After a couple of months they were going to flunk me out, and once again I felt that vulnerability—as if I'd fallen overboard into deep water. If I lose this, where am I? One more Black kid who can barely read, washing dishes on the island of Manhattan? "Not if I can help it," thought I. So, in desperation I conjured up a truly outrageous offer they couldn't refuse. I would become their janitor without pay if they would let me continue to study. After some brief negotiations, it was so agreed.

Things began to improve, and maybe even I began to improve. As an actor, that is. But when it came time to cast the first big student production, in walked a new guy, another kid from the Caribbean. Not a member of the group, but someone to whom the director had assigned the part I had secretly hoped to get. After all my studies, busting my butt trying to learn to act, not to mention busting my butt sweeping the walk and stoking the furnace, she cast him in the lead. Well, I had to admit, he was a pretty good-looking kid, and he had a good voice. He could even sing a little.

I tried to find some consolation in the fact that they made me his understudy. But little did I know, on the night of the first major run-through, the one night an important director was coming to watch the show, the other Caribbean kid who had been cast for the lead—a kid named Harry Belafonte—couldn't make it. I had to go on for him and, son of a gun, the visiting director liked what I did, and he called me in to audition for a play he was planning to present on Broadway.

"I'm opening *Lysistrata* on Broadway," he said. "There might be a small part you could try out for, if you're available."

"Are you kidding?" I thought to myself.

Next thing you know, five weeks later, on opening night, I'm staring out from a Broadway stage onto a sea of white faces in a packed theater—staring back at me—scared beyond belief as I fumbled unsuccessfully for my lines.

The word "bad" cannot begin to accommodate my wretchedness. I mean, I was *bad*. The stage fright had me so that I was giving the wrong cues, jumbling the lines, and within an instant the audience was rolling in the aisles.

The moment the scene I was in came to its torturous end, it was time for this Caribbean kid to run for cover. My career was over before it had begun, and the void was opening up once again to receive me. I didn't even go to the cast party, which meant that I wasn't around when the first reviews appeared.

The critics trashed the show. I mean, they hated it. But they liked me. I was so godawful they thought I was good. They said they admired my "fresh, comedic gift."

If you saw this in an old black-and-white movie on TV, would you believe it? Someone was looking out for me, for sure.

My "triumph" in *Lysistrata* leads immediately to an understudy's job in the touring company of *Anna Lucasta*. Then after a long, lean, and frustrating period I found out, quite by accident, that 20th Century Fox was about to begin casting for a movie called *No Way Out*. That, as it turned out, was my first motion picture job. Fifty years and fifty-six movies later, here I am recalling the year, the day, the words, and the resolve that forged a new and undreamed-of beginning and launched a journey more incredible than I could have imagined—through the streets of New York, along the highways and byways of life, on to a destiny written in a time before I came, by hands other than my own.

THE UNIVERSITY OF THE WEST INDIES GALA

At a 2001 gala hosted by the American Foundation for the University of the West Indies at the New York Marriott Marquis hotel, Sidney received the university's Legacy Award, an honor conferred annually to notable individuals who have attained high levels of achievement. In its official statement, the UWI cites "the career and achievements of this cultural icon. His legendary performances and outspoken support of civil rights have left an indelible mark on the Caribbean and the world. As one of the most visible Black role models, Poitier carried the hopes and inspiration of an entire people. His films never shied away from addressing sensitive issues of race." Harry Belafonte, a past Legacy Award recipient, was the event's honorary patron.

Ladies and gentlemen,

In troubled times when spoken words lose their power, nature does not grow silent. The language of the heart still speaks, and the language of the soul responds. In troubled times when words fail to light our way, nature's primal memory sends instinct to guide us in the dark and lead us toward the light. And so it is that we are here tonight in honor of that which instinct tells us needs no apologies and never needs to be excused: integrity!

Integrity is more than a word. It is more than an element independently floating high above us, waiting for someone or something to elevate itself within range of its touch.

It is not a condition called into existence by words imaginatively arranged. It is not a compliment, nor a distinction ceremoni-

[Integrity] is almost always found side by side with character or shoulder to shoulder with decency; step by step it moves alongside fidelity, honesty, selflessness, and compassion.

ously bestowed by the state. It is an accompaniment. It never comes out of thin air; it always travels in close company with other forces. It is almost always found side by side with character or shoulder to shoulder with decency; step by step it moves alongside fidelity, honesty, selflessness, and compassion. It is always there to heal when dignity is stripped from human life and trampled on with calculated disregard.

The University of the West Indies is accompanied here tonight by the personal integrity that has characterized all the years of her useful and productive life. These two, the University of the West Indies and integrity, have seen each other through troubled times, through pain and sorrow, through joy and happiness. They have come to be with us tonight with an enviable record of good deeds in their wake, so that we can salute them for their presence in so many lives being lived at the margins and for striking such sparks as will enlighten the brain and broaden the mind.

To you, the University of the West Indies, and your companion traveler, our thanks and appreciation for the great good you are doing in the nation-states of the Caribbean and the rest of the world.

As to tonight—congratulations to all concerned with this most wonderful, well-designed evening. More need not be said; further words would only lose their power! Thank you.

THE UNIVERSITY OF SOUTHERN CALIFORNIA SCHOOL OF CINEMA-TELEVISION COMMENCEMENT

Sidney was a founding member of the University of Southern California School of Cinema-Television Board of Councilors (renamed the School of Cinematic Arts in 2006), serving alongside George Lucas, Steven Spielberg, David Geffen, and others. In May 2000, he spoke at the film school's commencement ceremonies at the Shrine Auditorium in downtown Los Angeles.

Class of 2000, I am pressed by conscience to admit that when I first received your most generous invitation to come and speak, I was troubled by the thought of what could I possibly have of interest to say to an educated, well-rounded, young, awesomely cool class like you.

I've not been, to my satisfaction, fully able to put that thought to rest. In fact, while waiting to be introduced a few minutes ago, the grounds for my earlier concern intensified as it gradually became clear that your presence here, indeed, speaks of quick minds, keen interest, vibrant curiosities, and expectations that threaten to keep me on my toes and make me reach beyond my grasp.

All of which gives rise to more than a little nervousness. Because if you are, in fact, all those things—quick and curious and expectant—it means I will have to struggle to measure up, so that you won't have to measure down. I would hate that.

Talking to people that much smarter than I is, first, risky! Because my ignorance will have no place to hide from your computer-fast minds listening for historical truths, philosophical gems, political insights, spiritual resonances, and errors of grammar. Forget it! You won't hear any of those. Errors of grammar are about all you are likely to get. Second, it flies in the face of logic! Because, class of 2000, you, at your age, know at least fifty times more than I knew when I was your age. So, what could I say? What should I say? Well, I decided whatever I say, I will speak it only to you. Parents, faculty, and friends can listen in if they want. But my remarks will be from me directly to you, class of 2000.

Pride in this school's long and honored tradition of providing nurture for the development and growth of civilized society is never more exemplified than on days like this, when the labor of teachers and students, faculty and parents is harvested and made ready to lend itself to the process of continuance, to the widening, deepening, and extending of both civilized society and the opportunities this institution believes will be waiting for you, the class of 2000.

In each of the generations of filmmakers who have gone before you, there were those who came with visions so unique as to set new standards in their time. No need, in these brief remarks, to identify them by name, by profession, or by contribution, since their bodies of work have been preserved and stand in witness to their history, fact by fact. It is, therefore, undeniable that your ambitions, and mine, were stirred and shaped by impressions left on each of us by the power of their gifts.

Today, class of 2000, if, by chance, you feel obliged by your creative passion to reach beyond them—to raise the level of the bar yet another notch in your time, through your life's work—let me tell you, that's a good sign.

Class of 2000, if restless expectations are thrashing about inside you in anticipation of what the future holds, that's a good sign. If you are already searching and listening for hints as to when and where you might cross paths with that defining moment, that window of opportunity through which you and your talent will burst upon the world—maybe tomorrow, maybe next week, maybe next month—that's a good sign.

Class of 2000, you are poised at the edge of new beginnings, your journey ready to take wings. Precisely as the clouds of my journey's end are gathering up ahead. Because the time has come when the aged and weakened wings of my generation's journey can no longer hold their own against the wind. If you see that as fact, and that fact as one of life's unending processes, that's a good sign.

Class of 2000, this is the day the decks are cleared. This is the day you position yourselves for what tomorrow brings. There can be no better time than now, filled as you are with the satisfaction that always comes after a giant step has been taken, no better moment to take one last look back, across the many books you've cracked, the many hours you've logged, the many lessons you've learned, the many lectures you've internalized, the many facts you've unearthed, the many tiny bits of knowledge that have captured your imagination. I advise you to look closely. And if you spot genuine moments of clarity, flashes of insight, and pearls of wisdom, that's a good sign. Make note of them now, and chances

> *There can be no better time than now, filled as you are with the satisfaction that always comes after a giant step has been taken, no better moment to take one last look back, across the many books you've cracked, the many hours you've logged, the many lessons you've learned, the many lectures you've internalized, the many facts you've unearthed, the many tiny bits of knowledge that have captured your imagination.*

are they will return to warm your heart at seventy-three.

Now, be forewarned and not misled by what you've heard me say. I've not come to stroke you; I've come to challenge you. And if I am successful, you will recognize glimpses of yourselves somewhere in the remarks to follow. None of which is gospel, most of which even I have somehow managed to survive, but not without the hands of unseen forces being

somewhere in the details. However, since serendipity, providence, luck, karma, and other such intangibles can never be directed by our hands and must forever lie outside of our control, you must, yourselves, be responsible for setting the goals, choosing the route, and staying the course. Only you can articulate the distance you are willing to travel to become the "you" you want to be at seventy-three—and me, the "me" I'd like to be at 103. Clearly, I'm not altogether done yet.

If you agree that, for each of us, our journey's distance from where we are to where we want to be can best be measured by the size of our will and the passion of our intent, that's a good sign.

I now invite you to join me in an objective look at the moment at hand. If you see the fact of my standing here and you sitting there as being pregnant with implications, imageries, obligations, possibilities, and promises, that is a good sign. There are differences between us, you and I. Certainly more than meet the eye. There is a space between us—a distance, a divide. After all, I am seventy-three and you are in your golden twenties and thirties. Which obliges me to suggest you be ever mindful of the fact that life is tough, damn right!

Especially for those of us who tend to sit or stand on one of life's corners too long. However hard we look, we will never see as far as we should. However long we watch, we will seldom comprehend as clearly as we could.

However much talk we hear of wonder, we will seldom experience her touch. The narrowest view life will ever offer of itself is reserved for those of us who never venture forth, who never travel those unknown roads. Life knows who we are. She also knows where we are. But she rarely comes looking for those of us who are at the heart of ourselves, spectators. Her engines are not fired by us.

The narrowest view life will ever offer of itself is reserved for those of us who never venture forth, who never travel those unknown roads.

She instead waits anxiously for the coming of the curious traveler to whom she offers no guarantee that one road will lead to another; no promise that we won't get lost, as surely we will from time to time; no promise that we won't find ourselves abandoned where disaster of some unimaginable kind waits, and there be left to stand our ground with only instinct for guidance and trial and error for judgment. Left to perish or prosper. Alone. Deserted. Life is tough! Damn right!

She knows curiosity sharpens instinct. Instinct invites trial and error. Trial and error produce experiences. And experiences are the only armor, the only protection, she provides for those travelers who will spend their days on beckoning, unknown roads that pull at their curiosity. If you feel you can summon the resolve necessary to stand firm in the face of all life's challenges, with no guarantees, that's a good sign.

Class of 2000, on the reasonable chance that there may be those among you who might well be wondering, "Who is this seventy-three-year-old Sidney Poitier guy from a time we never knew . . . ?" Well, in the time you never knew, I earned my living these many years past as an actor and director in theater and films. I'm approaching the glow of a distant sunset, accompanied by the shadow of my accumulated years in which a reasonable number of unknown roads have pulled at such curiosity as I have had. I've come to see where you are, and to tell you where I've been and what I've seen, in case your journey takes you over ground I've covered. And it too can be said, I've come to learn what you can teach me.

When we are done with each other this day, I hope it will have been for good and sound reasons that we came together at this particular point in our lives. Coming as we have from different times, from different places, on different journeys, in different directions. While we each, you and I, have arrived at this moment burdened with the complexities of generational differences, I sincerely hope we discover a small patch of common ground on which we may stand and share in this short time we have as we pass each other by—my generation heading towards its final years, and your generation towards the arena where the game of life is played.

Whoever you are, however old you are—twenty years old at the threshold, seasoned traveler deeper in the journey, or the curious traveler seeking out, along some unknown road, the mysteries hidden in himself—know that I come with the weight of such accumulation as my spent years have left me. Experiences, burdens, victories, flaws, failures, inadequacies, disappointments, accomplishments, obligations, regrets, success, mistakes, and, worst of all, a heart that has been broken more than a few times. Yes, as you can clearly see, the shadows of my deeds are etched upon my face, along with the other requisite scars of survival. Indeed, I stand as proof positive that the wear and tear on the body, the mind, the spirit, and the soul is inescapable after such a long time in the arena of life. No matter what you're thinking now, trust me, you're not going to look any better than us when time, one day, finally delivers you where we once stood, facing, as you must, the distant sunset of your own years. This is how one comes to be, as one's journey winds down. If you have had glimpses of yourselves in the foregoing scenario, that's a good sign. In a time you never knew, standards were set. Planted deep in the discipline you have chosen. Where roots took hold and left markers of excellence.

And now, as your journey begins, they're waiting to test your measure, to see your stuff, observe your style; looking to see how well you do at keeping instinct and intuition out of the abusive reach of convenience, as you come with decades yet unspent, with which to deal. Challenges you haven't dreamed of are waiting for you. If you feel that it is in your nature to rise to each of them, show them your stuff, declare that—driven by will and intent—you've come to leave your mark, plant your vision, and set new standards. If that be the ground you intend to cover over the distance of your journey, let me tell you, class of 2000, that's one hell of a good sign. Good luck. And Godspeed.

COSTCO SCHOLARSHIP FUND BREAKFAST

The Costco Scholarship Fund raises money for students of color to attend college, with scholarship money split evenly between Seattle University and the University of Washington. Sidney was chosen to be the keynote speaker at the second annual scholarship breakfast, which many local notables attended, including then Washington governor Gary Locke and Seattle's first African American mayor (1990-1998), Norm Rice, who introduced Sidney. The event took place on September 20, 2001—just days after the 9/11 attacks, to which his speech refers.

I cannot recall having ever been so suddenly and deeply placed in the debt of others. First by an irresistibly seductive invitation from a great American company, and now by that wonderful introduction from Norm Rice, former mayor of a great American city. I am honored by both.

A tip of the cap—and a special salute to the university and the Costco company for their steadfast commitment to the enhancement of American education. To you, ladies and gentlemen, who together make up this combined audience of their rock-solid supporters, my heartfelt appreciation and thanks for your presence here this morning.

Welcome. As the monumentally catastrophic events of the past ten days so painfully demonstrated, America's future, the preservation of her values, and the unbending strength of her resolve can only be assured if the quality of education her children and her children's children receive is second to none, the world over. There is no getting around that. We cannot leap over it, we cannot burrow under it, we cannot sidestep it. There is no way around it. We must collect our resources, test our will, face the challenge, and persevere.

The university knows it and the Costco company knows it. Their combined efforts speak directly to America's future, its children, and the quality of their education. But most of all, the scholarship recipients of these awards know it—they have collected their resources, tested their will, stand ready to face the challenge and, moreover, persevere. To them we all say congratulations. America—the future—the world awaits you.

My remarks this morning will not be about education, however, but rather about a matter of personal concern that involves you and me and revolves around three facts. Which, simply and honestly put, are:

Fact one—Who am I? Who is this person you have so kindly consented to come visit with and listen to what he has to say?

Fact two—You know to some degree what I do for a living, therefore you know of me. But . . .

Fact three—Sad to say, you don't know me—the baby, the boy, the young man, the person who existed before celebrity happened by.

Almost always when an honor is bestowed upon a well-known celebrity personage, that celebrity personage receives it, is roundly applauded for receiving it, and in turn offers all the thank-yous for having been given it. While the little-known person at the heart of the transaction, standing with the weight of accumulated hardships on his shoulders, gathered over years of a complex life, lived between the margins of trial and error, is overlooked. Not acknowledged. In fact, remains virtually nonexistent.

Well, enough of that. This morning you are going to be introduced to that little-known person at the core of this transaction—the real me, that Sidney Poitier who is the bedrock foundation of that other fellow, that celebrity personage person, who is, traditionally, always out front, in the public's eye, grabbing all the attention, all the goodies. Let me tell you! The real me is sick of it.

To begin with, ladies and gentlemen, long before celebrity happened by, the real me that you don't know and that might likely shock you could have best been seen through the eyes of my mother. So let's start from back there, and keep an eye on the fact that no celebrity personage was anywhere in sight when the hard stuff of life was taking her measure.

Evelyn Outten was her maiden name. She was born on October 22, 1896. She married a guy named Reggie. I was born to her on February 20, 1927. She was instinctual in her nurturing, her discipline, her molding. I was a restless boy with a fair amount of imagination and no common sense. But she never gave up. It was in her nature, her personality, to work on me using what was natural to her: the *whap! whap!* method.

On those days when my misbehavior and her tolerance were out of sync, she would wave a finger at my head, saying, "That thick skull of yours—what's up there?" *Whap!*

"Not one thimble full of common sense that I can see." *Whap!*

One day when I was nine years old, preoccupied with whatever fun thing had hold of my imagination, she called for me: "Sidney."

Sidney referred to his parents, Reginald James Poitier and Evelyn Outten Poitier, often in his speeches. Tomato farmers in the Bahamas, they and their hard work, love for their children, and high moral standards left a lasting impression on their famous son.

Annoyed at the intrusion I said, "What? I'm busy."

I didn't see the slap coming. *Whap!* It lifted me off my feet and dumped me on my back. That was discipline—instant and direct. No explanation, no discussion—*whap!* And I got the point. Next time she said "Sidney," I said, "Yes, Mama, what would you like me to do for you?"

But I still didn't know what fear was until the time when my mother caught me and my eight-year-old niece playing doctor. No one else was home—my mother was on her way to the store, but she had forgotten her purse and doubled back. She walked in and there we were. We knew instantly that we were going to die. We were on the floor, and we knew for sure that was where our corpses would be found by the rest of the family. She stood over us adjusting herself into an attack mode. There was absolute silence in the room.

My niece and I knew that one word from us and two violent deaths from shredding would occur. We've seen her do it—with chickens we had just said goodbye to, only hours before. They wound up on Sunday's dinner table. So, we just looked at her. Then we started looking at each other. At the same moment, we each decided it would be better if she only kills one of us—so we both tried with subtle body language to get it across to her that it was the other one's fault.

It didn't work. My niece started to cry. I thought that was a damn good move. So, I started to cry. Until my mother said, "Don't gimme that—just shut right up! Right now!" At that moment, my niece and I both knew we were onto something—and started crying louder and harder. That maneuver, born of desperation, went a long way in helping us dodge a major bullet.

To further illustrate the effects of my mother's nurturing and molding: when I was ten years old, I wrote a sexy love letter to an eleven-year-old girl. I signed my name, folded it neatly, and passed it to her when no one was looking and waited anxiously, overnight, for what I expected the next day would be a favorable response. She showed it to her mother—who showed it to my mother—who called out to me, "Sidney—bring that thick skull of yours over here." Unaware that I had been busted, I didn't expect what I should have been expecting. As I entered her strike zone I said, "Yes, Ma . . ." That's as far as I got.

Whap!

I didn't see that slap coming either. Among the useful things I learned from that endeavor was that if my mother was really that fast with her hands, I was looking at brain damage in the very near future. Certainly, as you might expect, I have written love letters since then, but you won't find my signature on any of them!

Bit by bit one learns; bit by bit one pays. By the way, guess who was conspicuously absent during those trials and tribulations: that celebrity personage fellow, of course! But let's not even go there. Now where was I . . . oh yes! Get a load of this.

I was one of seven children—two girls and five boys—of whom I was the last of the lot, the most incorrigible of the lot, and the most vulnerable of the lot . . . considering that my brothers and my sisters had entered into an unholy alliance to starve me to death while I was still a baby. Example: dinnertime! With the seven of us seated around the kitchen table, my mother would dish a portion of the food onto each child's plate. Everything was cool as long as Mother was in the kitchen. The second her back was turned, my food was gone. If she stepped out of the kitchen for a matter of seconds, by the time she returned my food would be in six other stomachs. Not one bite could I salvage.

If I could have talked, I would have said to them, "Where is your moral fiber? Where is your sense of solidarity in this family's struggle for survival? What would the gossipmongers say if they got wind of this sort of ethically edgy and morally indefensible goings-on in a good Christian family? The Bible says be kind, caring, and charitable to your neighbor. I'm more than a neighbor; I'm your baby brother—who can't talk or walk yet! But just you wait, you heathens! The day I wake up and I'm able to talk, your ass is grass—all of you. I will testify against you in a court of law in a minute. And I'll visit you all in jail. And I'll sit there eating all kinds of scrumptious mouthwatering stuff while you watch me through a plastic partition, drooling, while I eat, and eat, and eat." Except, of course, any recently departed chicken of my acquaintance. That is probably what I would have said to them if I could have talked.

If it's beginning to become clear to you that mine was not a normal life, then we are on the right track. For example, from the moment I was born, I have lived a very . . . a very . . . I'm searching for the right word. "Unusual" doesn't fit. "Strange" is too mild. "Wild" is too tame. "Weird" isn't perfect, but it does just about cover it.

Yes! I have lived a very weird life, which ranged from interesting to unbelievable, to scary, to shocking, to earth-shattering circumstances that cannot be called by any other name than earth-shattering circumstances. How I survived will test your firmest grip on logic and reason, unless you leave room in your calculation for the possibility that maybe God was in the details. Don't be surprised if you come upon an undiscovered miracle or two, somewhere in my seventy-four years.

Under normal circumstances, you might be led to believe, given what I've said to now, that I am a fiction writer. I am not. The proof is in the living, the lessons were in the journey, paid for each day, each hour of those seventy-four years—while the man that I am was being built from inside the boy that I was, woven thread by thread, moment by moment, out of youthful restlessness, a medium-sized ego, a fair amount of imagination, and no common sense. Yep, no getting around it. To that point I had lived a really, really weird life—and it got weirder. How much weirder? You judge for yourself. Here, let me run by you a few examples that come to mind—each experience no more, no less than a building block in the overall life that I have lived.

By the time my best friend, Fritz, and I were ten years old in the village where we were raised, our status as Romeos among the girls of the village was pitiful. In fact, we were off the charts altogether; our best efforts registered nothing. Not even a blip. No impact, no impression, no recognition. It was common practice for the girls to look right past us. Our popularity needed a major spike. So, under the weight of social embarrassment, our egos at low ebb, we turned to mystical folklore for remedy. We resolved to win the hearts of the two most unobtainable girls in the village, by following step-by-step accounts embedded in local mythology, which spoke of magical powers that can be found in the soul of a frog and be transferred to someone who wants to win the love of the girl of his dreams. Surefire results were promised when the recipe and the ritual were followed faithfully.

Took Fritz and I a couple of days to prepare. First, we had to ambush two frogs. Then, we had to get two small matchboxes, place a frog in each box, bury the two boxes one foot underground—on a moonlit night—and wait for a certain number of weeks to pass. In the meantime, we had to obtain a strand of hair from the head of each girl. That was a tricky maneuver, almost got us killed, definitely got us viewed as psychologically impaired and just plain nuts.

But we pressed on anyway, then we dug up the boxes, in which we found only the skeleton remains of our two volunteers. Among the bones in each box was a bone in the shape of a V. We each took the hair of the girl of our dreams, wrapped it around one branch of the V, then we each wrapped a strand of

our own hair around the other branch of the V, replaced the V's in their respective matchboxes and waited to rebury them—as prescribed by the ritual—at precisely the moment a full moon was directly overhead, and the ghosts of ancient sailors could be seen dancing on the waters.

Five days later we started looking for telltale signs of behavioral changes in the girls of our dreams. On the sixth day, as promised in the accounts, we should have started picking up faint smiles here and there. Best-case scenario, by the end of ten days they would not be able to keep their eyes off us.

Results: nothing happened. The girls still looked right past us to the hotshot Romeos who had already captured their hearts. The recipe and the ritual changed nothing. Except to this day, Fritz and I are still not spoken well of in the frog community.

At twelve years old, I had my first encounter with alcohol. It was provided by three of my friends, in the same age range, who had just stolen a case of rum. With the help of myself and two other friends of the same age, that case of rum was hoisted up and over the twelve-foot-high wall of an abandoned estate. There we settled in the overgrown bushes of that estate and drank two bottles of that rum. Straight up. No chaser. Our mouths were on fire. The fire raced down our throats, blew out our esophaguses, raged through our stomachs, circled around in our small intestines, and then headed straight for our brain. We were all smashed in five minutes—and that's where the trouble started.

We couldn't climb back over the wall. It took us six hours to sober up enough to make it. That fateful event would leave an indelible impact on the lives of six twelve-year-old boys. Ten years later, three of us will have died of alcoholism. Two would remain trapped in moderate consumption for years before they too would succumb. That other fellow—that celebrity personage person—wasn't around to lend a hand that time, either. Meanwhile, however, for reasons known somewhere in the universe, I escaped. It appears there was someone sitting on my shoulder, and other encounters were waiting up ahead.

I spent three nights in three different jails, for three different reasons, in three different parts of the world—one in the Caribbean, one in Florida, and one in New York City. The details will catch you by surprise, but you'll have to read the book to get the full flavor. That other fellow is reluctant to speak about such things, embarrassed by the fact that life is not always tidy and that unmanageable moments are visited upon us and leave us no choice but to struggle back from defeat.

On six different occasions, death and I were within a hair's breadth of a final embrace. How many forces had to be in perfect balance for us to pass so closely, so many times? Were they random, serendipitous

forces? Or were they under the guidance of energies unknown? And could the answer be more than human understanding can embrace, forever leaving us free to make what we will of such mysteries?

One last thing about my mother. In the early evening of February 20, 1927, I was born to her in a nondescript, clapboard house in the colored section of Miami, Florida, more than two months prematurely. Before the following day had run its course, my chances for survival were reduced to levels at which no reasonable chance remained. With the exception of my mother, everyone—including my dad—was preparing to let me go. In fact, my father, who had already lost several children to disease and stillbirth, was somewhat stoical about the situation. From the sight of me he wasn't at all sure there was enough there to take hold—an assessment shared by almost all who were witness to my entrance into this life. Thus, my father left the house the following morning for a stroll that ended up at the local undertaker's parlor, in a discussion centered around preparations for my burial. Later, he returned to the house with a shoebox that was to serve as a miniature casket for my remains.

My mother stood alone against the prevailing opinion, which had by then reluctantly agreed to write me off. She rose from her bed, dressed herself, and set out from the house in desperate search of whatever support she could gather. The reservoir of

Sidney with Joanna and daughters Sydney and Anika. He spoke at length about his remarkable life in this inspirational speech to students of color.

hope in that unsophisticated woman from a different culture battled against despair, hour after hour, over a long and fruitless day. Then, as a last resort, when night began to fall and she had nowhere else to turn, she visited a reader of palms, a diviner of tea leaves: the local soothsayer. The two women sat down at a table and looked at each other.

After some intense gazing back and forth and much silence, the soothsayer closed her eyes and took my mother's hand. There was more silence, an uncomfortably long silence, and then the soothsayer's face began to twitch. Her eyes rolled back and forth behind her lids. Strange sounds began to gurgle up from her throat. Then, all at once, her eyes flew open again and she said, "Don't worry about your son. He will survive and he will not be a sickly child. He will grow up to be . . . He will travel to most of the corners of the earth . . . He will walk with kings. He will be rich and famous. Your name will be carried all over the world. You must not worry about that child."

So, for fifty cents, my mother found the support she needed for backing a long shot. She came home and ordered my father to remove the shoebox casket from the house—there would be no need for it. And so it followed, for reasons that my mother believed were better left unquestioned, that I pulled through.

She is gone now—and while it is impossible for her to be with us here tonight in person, she is here in presence. So in the course of the day, whenever you sense her in the vicinity of your thoughts and feelings, be at ease. Listen to her life and search through her sixty-eight years for such pearls of wisdom as might have been left behind on the roadway of her existence, in case your journey takes you over ground she's covered.

My restlessness, her *whap! whap!* discipline, her no-nonsense nurturing and molding, shaped my boyhood years, which served as the foundation on which this life would eventually be built.

I am now no longer eleven years old. Bit by bit I learned and bit by bit I paid. The seventy-four years, six months, and some days since my birth have forged the child that I was into the man that I am—here at the other end of the spectrum, here where I now stand, a person in his advanced years looking back across a lifetime to see what he remembers. Some memories stay close to the heart for easy recollection. Others wander away, leaving only ghosts of their reflections that grow dimmer year by year until they fade away, to forever be forgotten by the youthful heart that kept them warm.

Yes, much of what we were slips away. Some of which, not altogether unnoticed. Year by year, you have the feeling something else is missing—more each year than the year before. The fact is, day by day, the members of my generation are all getting closer to that final bend in the road, can't escape it. There is a "there" there. And we'll each reach "there" if we stay on course. And we're destined to do just that.

I've noticed changes in myself in recent years. A tiny bit of slowing down, physically and mentally. When I had my first half a dozen senior moments it scared the daylights out of me. Now they don't bother me at all. I find myself saying to my closest friends, "What did you say your name was again?"

I don't fret about it none. In fact, it put my friends at ease and got them talking about how their first senior moments scared the stuffing out of them, their first time around. Yes, I remember well how quick I was of body, how sharp of mind. Time was, the doorbell would ring—I would bounce up, streak out of my den, through the living room, across the hall, and at the door in no time. Now the doorbell rings—first, I think about it. Then I crank myself up and get there when I can. If they couldn't wait, that's their problem.

There are a lot of things I can't do like I used to. Good thing about that is, I can't remember half of them. Things like that remind you that you are getting on. The other morning, I bent down and tied my shoes— then realized I didn't even have them on.

My eyes seem to be getting better—which, I am told, is a sure sign of how far gone I am. My hearing, too, has been acting funny. I see lips moving, but I can't hear what the hell they are saying. And don't mention my nose! You know how people say, "So and so has a nose for something"? My nose shuts down for the whole winter, when there's not even one pollen molecule anywhere in the whole country, then suddenly in the spring, it starts running like a river. My hairline is retreating towards the back of my neck. There is no longer any warranty covering any of my moving parts. But hey—in the final analysis, it doesn't matter how many times you've been knocked down. What matters is what you do with your time after you get up. So let us move on. What the hell! Who knows? Maybe the best is yet to come—and a second waltz awaits us, in a place we could never imagine.

I know many of you are wondering about the Hollywood years, the miraculous career, which became such a major part of this weird life of mine. There is much about that part of my journey that draws the interest, the curiosity, of many people, my own included. The next time we meet, I promise to lead you further into that unbelievable journey that took me from the tumultuous, untamed, out-of-control, runaway roller coaster that you now have come to know as my boyhood years, to fifty-one years as a principal player in American motion pictures.

In concluding, allow me to say that it is my wish that, for you, this evening has blended the boy that I was, the journey that I made, and the man that I am—including that celebrity personage person—into the full picture of a meaningful life. A man that you know! If so, then much credit is due to Evelyn Outten Poitier for her nurturing, her discipline, and her molding . . . and for never giving up on me.

Thank you, ladies and gentlemen, for the opportunity to introduce my total self to you—and thank you for your kind attention.

SAINT MARK'S SCHOOL COMMENCEMENT

Later in his life, Sidney was often self-deprecating in public speeches—especially when it came to addressing young people. "Who is this grandfatherly-looking guy?" he would ask in a tongue-in-cheek manner, and then explain that he, too, was once a boy and had experienced many of the same challenges and emotions that kids in twenty-first-century America go through—albeit on an island in the Bahamas. In June of 2002, he was invited to speak at the Saint Mark's School in Altadena, California, by his friend Reveta Bowers, a local leader in education with whom Sidney served on the board of directors of the Walt Disney Company. This speech to the young graduates of the Episcopal day school is emblematic of his values and full of encouragement for a new generation. In line with his philosophy of self-improvement, he urges these sixth graders to pursue education and explore their curiosities, so that they can someday be "grandfatherly" in age and wisdom, too, and look back on their own lives with contentment.

Class of 2002, I am delighted to be here.

That sentence is a comment, a remark, an expression that might trigger a question in your mind. Why is this grandfatherly-looking guy so delighted to be here? Is he really delighted to be here, or is he just saying that? And if he is just saying that, what is his motive for saying that? Has he a relative graduating? Did a parent or teacher ask him to come do this? If any of you are having such a thought, you got me: a parent did ask me—a parent who is a very good friend of mine, and a very good friend of the school.

But!

That's not why I'm delighted to be here. I'm delighted to be here because this grandfatherly-looking guy has inside of him the twelve-year-old boy he used to be, and he—that twelve-year-old boy—is absolutely delighted to be here. You don't know this yet, but inside every grandfatherly-looking guy, there's a twelve-year-old who never ever goes away—as you will discover over the next sixty to one hundred years.

Now, since like you I'm twelve years old, and I'm the graduation speaker, I would like to invite you to join me in examining that inescapable and very often annoying human habit some people have of always sizing up other people. Yuck. As a twelve-year-old, I have always had a problem with that. This morning I would like to look that practice straight in the eye, not be intimidated by it, and put it behind me. For all of my twelve years, I've been a little ill at ease with the process of sizing up and being sized up. I hate being sized up. And since it's not possible to hide from it, I want you to help me face it.

It starts when one's a baby. If you're cute, they say, "You're so cute." If you're not cute, they say, "You're so cute." Why don't they leave each other alone? What are they looking for? When they do that, well, old grandfatherly guys say they know what everybody is looking for when they size a person up. They're looking for signs, for information, for hints, for patterns of behavior on which to base a judgment as to what kind of a person a person is. Grandfatherly guys say it's not a bad thing, sizing up. On the contrary, they say sizing up is a useful and necessary tool provided by nature for assessing danger, opportunity, friendliness, love, affection, ambition, reliability, trustworthiness, compassion, shyness, self-doubt, self-worth, self-respect, strength of character, complexity, substance, power of will, and intent of purpose.

Speaking for myself, I don't like sizing up—especially when it comes to the glittering whims of the pop youth culture: who's popular, who's not, who's the jock, who's in the "in crowd," who rejects you, puts you down for some stupid reason, doesn't like the way you look, the way you dress, who are mean to your friends . . . I think sizing people up like that sucks. But for some reason, that old grandfatherly guy I've become keeps trying to get me to size up myself. Even now he's

Assess yourself, acquaint yourself with your own levels of friendliness, ambition, reliability, trustworthiness, compassion, shyness, self-doubt, self-respect, strength of character, complexity, substance, power of will, and intent of purpose.

saying to me, "Do it, do it." Don't be afraid. Assess yourself, acquaint yourself with your own levels of friendliness, ambition, reliability, trustworthiness, compassion, shyness, self-doubt, self-respect, strength of character, complexity, substance, power of will, and intent of purpose. "It is in that arena we must define our self," says the old grandfatherly guy that I've become, "and not seek self-definition among the glittering whims of a passing pop youth culture."

Shoot for character, friendliness, compassion, opportunity; aim for a fair-minded appraisal of self and respect for the effort of others. If you like what you find, nurture it; if you see room for improvement, fill it. Since people are going to size us up whether we like it or not, let's give them something to shoot for. Let's give them something to emulate. Let's show them the stuff we're made of. Let the world know that you are coming to plant your vision and leave your mark in the name of all that's fair and just in a civilized society. There is no better way for one to live one's life than in the service of all that is fair and just in a civilized society.

My twelve years were spent in a semi-primitive society, under primitive conditions, where fair and just were likewise the code for a useful, productive life. Let me give you an example of what my twelve years were like in that semi-primitive society and how I first came to see the unusual manner in which the code of fair and just were sometimes applied in unexpected ways.

I spent my twelve years on an island in the Caribbean. Cat Island was forty-six miles long and three to five miles wide. There were only about two hundred families on the whole island. The population of our village was about thirty to forty families. I had just one friend to play with, and he lived a long distance away. On the island there were no cars, no trucks, no buses, no trains, no paved roads, no electricity, no running water, no television, no ice cream, no movie houses. At night we used candlelight, firelight, or moonlight to get about to see where we were going. Night or day, everybody walked wherever they needed to go, or rode a horse or donkey if they were lucky enough to own one. In fact, there were stretches in my life when I was a kid when I would go for a whole week and never see a single soul other than my immediate family. As a result, some of my best friends were birds and lizards and frogs; some of my worst enemies were wasps, mosquitoes, sea urchins, and tarantula spiders. I used to have regular conversations with all of them.

On my end, I was really cool with being the boy that I was. Ours was a simple, uncomplicated relationship between a kid and his friends and his enemies. But something happened in the time between those boyhood years and today. On my side of those relationships, it seemed—as manhood approached—I became more and more aware of a gradual drifting away from the purity of those youthful days to distances further and further removed from simplicity. Until, sadly, I would lose track of my friends and my enemies from my early years, without whom I was left with no alternative but to turn and face the hard realities of grown-up survival, which immediately and routinely set about changing the rules of life as I had known them.

That is why—from the grandfatherly part of me—I highly recommend that you always remember that to each of us comes a time when we find ourselves in need of an honest look at how steady we are at the wheel of our own existence. Are we captains of our own ship? With a course set? A route planned? And a destination fixed? Or are we on uncertain seas, scrambling frantically to stay abreast of the winds of change in a world moving faster, day by day, leaving us with less and less time for meaningful living, less and less time at the helm of our own lives.

My parents and my teachers tried their best to teach me that whomever or whatever I encounter on the roadway of life, I should always begin with, and rely on, the simple truth as I have come to know it, out of the life that I have lived and the education I've received.

I leave you with this thought: stay on course towards a good, solid education, plan your route, fix your destination, and simple truths will lead you to wisdom and knowledge—long before you yourself become a grandfatherly-looking person, speaking to a generation yet unborn about the code of fair and just.

I leave you with this thought: stay on course towards a good, solid education, plan your route, fix your destination, and simple truths will lead you to wisdom and knowledge...

Thank you for the invitation to come and visit on this very special day. Congratulations to each of you, class of 2002.

THE BUCKLEY SCHOOL
FUNDRAISER

Sidney and Joanna's daughters Anika and Sydney both attended the Buckley School in Sherman Oaks, California—an independent coed school offering pre-K to twelfth grade education—with which the family continues to be involved. Sidney was a member of Buckley's board of trustees from 1988 to 1994 and gave the following talk at a November 2004 fundraising event.

For Joanna and me, the reflection of the Buckley School as seen through the lives of our children are among our most treasured memories. There they were, little people leaving home in the morning, returning in the afternoon knowing a little more than they did the day before about the big wide world in which they lived—a world filled with mystery and wonder and so much more that they could not yet understand. But, day in and day out at the Buckley School, discoveries of one kind or another would light up their innocent faces while quietly capturing their still very young imaginations. Some discoveries bolstered their self-confidence. Others posed small threats that loomed larger than the level of their understanding could recognize and dismiss. That was an early stage. Across the years, other discoveries have led to other stages and deeper understanding.

With the passage of time, Joanna and I have witnessed the evolution of our two little people into full-fledged adult human beings—who have discovered, to their parents' delight, that values learned at a place called Buckley are now a part of their life's foundation. As adults, they stand on principles that articulate who they are. They have reached the stage where they believe and accept the deeper understanding that convictions, firmly held, will somewhere along life's road test their strength of character. That they should expect, therefore, to swim against the tide sometimes. That they should expect integrity, honesty, fairness, dignity, and compassion to be in evidence in all of their undertakings. And question firmly, vigorously, the absence of any one of them.

With daughters Sydney and Anika, who attended the Buckley School

Their word is their bond.

They know that, as they did, the students following in their footsteps should expect to look their middle-aged dad in the eyes and tell him "thanks" for swimming as fast as he could, to keep them afloat. And to take Mom in their arms, share a tear, and let her know they appreciated it all. That, ladies and gentlemen, is the Buckley School Joanna and I knew and loved.

HFC SAN ANTONIO

As a struggling actor in New York City in the 1950s, Sidney found himself short of money at a critical moment: the impending birth of his second daughter, Pamela. In a story he often retold, he visited the Household Finance Corporation (HFC) on Fifty-Seventh Street and Broadway to take out a loan of seventy-five dollars—enough to cover the cost of delivery at Beth Israel Hospital—rather than accept a film role that he felt "simply didn't measure up." The character "didn't fight for what mattered to him most. He didn't behave with dignity." Sidney's moral resolve earned him the admiration of agent Marty Baum, who would become his longtime manager and friend. In the early 2000s, he was invited to speak at an HFC event in San Antonio, Texas.

Good morning, ladies and gentlemen. I am delighted to be here. My thanks and heartfelt appreciation for the gracious invitation you have extended to come visit with you on this special weekend—and the warm, welcoming manner in which I'm being received.

The last encounter I had with HFC was more than forty-five years ago—when you okayed a seventy-five-dollar loan to me. That was an important loan at that time in my life. And next week I'll be mailing you my very last payment on that loan—just kidding, guys, just kidding.

An unsophisticated young man with no substantive credentials walked in and laid down the best acting performance of his life—and you coughed up seventy-five bucks.

I took a risk, you took a risk, and we both stood tall.

Obligations assumed. Obligations fulfilled. I think your record will show I didn't miss a beat. We were each true to our word. Times have changed since then; you have grown bigger and more substantive, and I've grown older and more contemplative across these forty-five years. We both are different than we were. The world is different than it was. In the aftermath of recent events and their horrific impact on our senses, I have, like you, done a considerable amount of thinking about my family, my friends, my acquaintances, my country, my culture, my generation. The sum total of all that brain crunching amounted to an introspective look at self and that world in which we lived, until it unexpectedly changed on the morning of the eleventh of September, forcing me to check for structural damage at the very foundation of my self-perception. "Who am I? Who are you? Who are we?" I asked myself.

Searching for an answer led only to other questions—until I somehow came upon the realization that the answers I sought were hidden in a question I had not yet asked. "What is it I don't know about myself? What is it we don't know about each other?"

Here I am. Looking at you. You looking at me. At first glance, what do we see? We see only what first glances have the power to capture—the veneer of surface appearances. That, for the longest of times, was an early important lesson of nature, aimed at our intuitive sense of observation, taught by life, learned by us; then—over time, in the busyness of living—it would slowly be forgotten.

Tonight, in the painfully changed world we now know, that early important lesson is rapidly returning to memory with its ageless message still intact. Don't trust everything captured at first glance. Always try, instead, to look beyond "the veneer of surface appearances" through which too many of us "see" others of us without realizing that assumptions, snap judgments, and indifference obscure too, too much of who we really are—even to ourselves—and can add up to the corrosive dismissal of all that is price-

A publicity shot from Sidney's early career in Hollywood

less in a human life, when that human life is measured on the basis of surface appearances only.

When I was young in a time that has now passed, in a world that has now changed, before I had forgotten nature's lesson and its message, I often told myself and constantly reminded my children that when surface appearances become all we "see," they will consequently become all we "know"—of a place, a time, a circumstance, a people, an individual person, a self—causing us to miss all the fundamentals and their complexities

... when surface appearances become all we "see," they will consequently become all we "know"—of a place, a time, a circumstance, a people, an individual person, a self—causing us to miss all the fundamentals and their complexities and subtleties and nuances of that place, that time, that circumstance, that people, that individual person...

and subtleties and nuances of that place, that time, that circumstance, that people, that individual person . . . a person whose fears, whose doubts, whose demons, whose capacity for love, hate, compassion, and forgiveness—all of which, together, constitute the core of that individual person's human personality. All that he or she is, in fact, lies just outside of reach, behind surface appearances.

Among the important things I don't know about you—and among the important things we don't know about each other—are simple basic truths. Like how many twists and turns, ups and downs, ins and outs, how many yeses and nos, knockdowns and get-ups; how many promises made and broken, mostly to ourselves; how many times our reach has fallen short of our aim; how many times disappointments have kicked our butts; how many times in the game of survival did failure hold most of the winning hands? Lots of times for certain—in both my life and yours.

When my mind's eye comes to rest among such things as the answers to those questions, I will be within touching range of an understanding as to who I really am, who you really are, and collectively who we really are. I am here in the hope that the spirit of this evening will bring us closer to that understanding. To that end, I've brought along my complete life for you to "see"—as clearly as possible with as little reliance on surface appearances as I can manage. All that I was—my dreams, my hopes, my doubts, my fears, such as I am, my limitations, my shortcomings, my weaknesses, and all that I now understand myself to be. The good, the bad, the unworthy, the unfinished, the imperfect, the rotten, a work in progress. All of me—warts, blemishes, and all—is here for you to see and know.

SARAH LAWRENCE COLLEGE COMMENCEMENT

Sarah Lawrence bestowed Sidney with an honorary doctorate of humane letters at its sixty-fifth commencement in May 1994, the same year his daughter Anika graduated from the college. The honor was given "in recognition of his talent and vision, his determination and sense of purpose and, above all, his leadership in the struggle for justice, freedom, and the rights of all human beings." Presenting Sidney with his honorary doctorate was his *Paris Blues* costar Joanne Woodward, herself a recent graduate of Sarah Lawrence.

Thank you, President Ilchman, young ladies and gentlemen of the graduating class, your compatriots in the continuing student body, faculty members, parents, and friends, I welcome you to this long-awaited, very good afternoon.

Why do I presuppose that your presence here speaks of quick minds, keen interest, vibrant curiosities, and expectations that threaten to keep me on my toes and possibly force me to reach beyond my grasp? As I sat here waiting to be introduced to you, I discovered such a presupposition roaming my consciousness, darting in and out of the concerns of my mind—the net effect of which makes for more than a little nervousness. If you are, in fact, all those things, it means I will have to struggle to measure up, in order that you won't have to measure down. I would hate that.

Talking to people that much smarter than me is, first, risky! Because my ignorance will have no place to hide from your computer-rapid minds which will deconstruct each sentence of my remarks at the speed of light, looking for historical truths, philosophical gems, political insights, spiritual resonance, and errors of grammar. Save for the latter, you won't find any of those other things. Second, it flies in the face of logic! Because you are the ones who went to college; I didn't. You should be talking to me—and I wish you would. I could use it. Third, I don't know you—class of '94. Except for my daughter and a few of

Sidney with his daughter—and new Sarah Lawrence graduate—Anika Poitier

her friends, and of course some members of the faculty, I don't know who you people are. Come to think of it, I don't know who my daughter is, pursuant to some of the ideas she comes home with from this school. All these years I thought free speech meant something else altogether. I sent you a daughter; you are sending me a person who not only talks back, but also tells me where I went wrong. And goes on to suggest how I can redeem those ill-spent portions of my questionable life. What kind of receipt is that for $20,000 a year? Especially since do-it-yourself kits are available at Crown bookstores at $79.95 a pop. By the way, if you do, indeed, find errors of grammar in anything I've said or will say, don't worry your heads. My daughter will remind me for the next seven years of each and every one of them. Sarah Lawrence has taught her to be expressive of her feelings and her thoughts—almost exclusively to me. Mom wouldn't stand for that stuff. When she puts her foot down, the lip gets zipped. I wish I knew how to do that. Well, moving on . . . If, as I suspect, you are indeed smarter than me, then you will just have to live with it. So, here I am, as a result of your most generous invitation to come speak with you.

I am pressed by conscience to admit that when the invitation was first extended, I was troubled by the fact that I didn't really know the class of '94. Instantly apprehensions kicked in over whether or not I would be able to fashion a proper address. There I was, faced with two central questions for which I had no ready answer. To whom will I speak? And what will I say? The question "To whom will I speak" was provocatively loaded. Should I speak to the graduating students, whom I don't really know; or through the students to their parents—who I, likewise, don't really know; or possibly, through the parents to the larger community? After all, it is not altogether unthinkable that, to some extent, I would have here the opportunity to speak to the nation as a whole—modern communications being what they are.

After some earnest wrestling with the question, an acceptable premise was found on which a positive response to the invitation could be based. I would speak only to you, the graduating class. Parents, friends, and faculty can listen if they choose, but my remarks, I decided, should be strictly from me directly to the class of '94—whom I don't really know.

But what is research for, if not to unearth such hidden backstories as might exist behind unfamiliar personalities, mysterious events, or unstable formations?

To begin my research, I first spoke with those who had only a historical view of Sarah Lawrence and graduating classes past and present. Here are some comments: "off the wall," "eclectic," "weird," "unusual," "free-thinkers," "marchers to a different drummer," "destined to change the world," "thank God they're not running the country," "I pray to God they will be running the country," "fearless," "opinionated," "loudmouths," "need a bath," "eat too much pizza."

Next I spoke with two groups of alumni in California who straddled forty years of days like this. To them I posed the following: What is Sarah Lawrence? Some comments: "It's great. It's great. No, it's better." "It's a small factory for making great people." "We're a state of mind. And we're everywhere that matters." "A place like any other, except it's not." "I didn't go there, that was my sister." Then I asked of them: What are you doing in your life now, after Sarah Lawrence? Some comments: "Everything. Literally, everything." "Nothing, I'm vegetating intellectually. Giving my head a rest." "Not what I had in mind. But I'm happy." "Family, career, searching for the missing whatever." "I'm established. Roots are down, hopes are high, and I get paid for doing what I love most. Thank you, Sarah Lawrence."

Next, I spoke to members of the class of '94—my daughter and some of her friends. I asked: What are you as a result of Sarah Lawrence? "Why?" "What is Sarah Lawrence as a result of us? This was a give-and-take thing, you know." "The way you ask the question implies that Sarah Lawrence worked a magic on us. How about the magic we worked on Sarah Lawrence?" "Ask me that question after I get a job." "Wiser, more mature." "Less afraid." "I think I'm smarter, more handsome, and a sexier devil than I was when I first got here." "I like to think we left a mark on each other—Sarah Lawrence and us." "Confident. That's what this education did for me. Now I can't wait to get out there and do my thing." "Bottom line: we are the better for having had the experience."

Now that I know what I know about the class of '94—more than meets the eye, may I add—I have chosen precisely that: the "that" about you which does not readily meet the eye. The obvious has not escaped those of us who love you and, therefore, need no further acknowledgment. As the world can see, you too are experiencing a little nervousness on this very good afternoon. Plus, you are flushed with anticipation for and anxiety about tomorrow, loaded with relief that this day has finally arrived. But the "that" about you that doesn't meet the eye has captured my interest.

So let me begin by talking about fun, having a good time, and about a place you've never been. A stimulating, tantalizing, seductive, intense place sitting just to the east of your imagination and west of your dreams. Fun, good times, enjoyment. Sounds like Hollywood—life in the fast lane. But you know it's not. You know that Hollywood's disproportionate view of sex, drugs, violence, and assorted depravities are only a cheap distorted imitation. You know there is much more to the place I'm talking about than Hollywood has the courage to explore. The place of which I speak is, of course, "the real, real adult world" where there are no rewinds. Can't replay only the good times, no fast-forward to skip over the pain or leapfrog the hard choices. You go through once. You get through once. That's life and that's real. But you know that, and you're not terrified by change. Therefore, on this very good afternoon, as you are poised and ready to begin your journey on such beckoning, unknown roads as will pull at your curiosity, let us pause here for a look back, in respectful reflection, on what went into the making of this moment.

Let me remind you that from your first moment in kindergarten, preschool, Head Start, unknown roads lay in wait up ahead. You knew it then, and you know it now. Nothing has changed. You have picked up tons of information along the way. Yes. You have absorbed such experiences as are characteristic of early life. Yes. And on this day, at this moment, a feeling of satisfaction mingles with a sense of triumph. Yes. And beneath those feelings, deep down in the very center of you, pearls of wisdom in their earliest stages of development are taking form. Yes. Yet, nothing has changed. Unknown roads still lay in wait, and they don't always lead to moments like this on days like these. But you know that. Because there's more to you than meets the eye.

THIS BIG WORLD

While many of Sidney's speeches are a matter of public record—some even viewable today with a few taps on one's cell phone—others are lost to time. In the following case, his words have been preserved without any supporting context. Though we no longer have the specifics of this academic address, we feel it is important to share these words with the world given their universal value. They display both his unique perspective on education and his deep humility as "an unevenly educated person." The speech also offers a candid view into Sidney's mindset as a public speaker and iconic entertainment figure.

Good evening, ladies and gentlemen. My heartfelt appreciation and thanks to each of you for your presence here tonight. Likewise to the university for its most generous invitation, which was beautiful in its composition, plus very cordial and complimentary in its request. I was delighted to receive such an invitation. So delighted was I, in fact, that I paid little notice to the expectations an acceptance would set in motion. Instead, my attention was on the single phrase that comprised the invitation: "Come visit and say a few words on any subject of your choice that would advance the cause of education." That impressive collection of simple words instantly drew my admiration and engaged my thoughts. The motivation of my ego, on the other hand, based as it most often is in its own self-interest,

saw the invitation as a bonanza of opportunities and a wealth of compliments waiting to be claimed—to our mutual benefit— by a speedy acceptance from me. As egos by their nature tend to do, mine immediately sensed the presence of power and honor reaching out through those simple words to bestow themselves upon me, and of course, it. To my ego, the invitation smelled like a win-win situation for both of us. "Foreclose on the advantage," it whispered in my ear. "Shut out the alternative," it advised. "Lock in the benefits," it urged. "After all," it continued with emphasis, "few men are invited by such prestigious institutions as this to 'come visit and say a few words'—and more importantly be granted the prerogative to select the subject on which he will deliver those few words."

Was my ego applying a full-court press? Was it seriously lobbying me to commit? Damn right it was. I know my ego, and consequently spoke in defense of my point of view, which I thought to be a more rational interpretation of the invitation's intent. Result? There we stood—eye to eye, my ego and me—unable to see, eye to eye, on an issue as uncomplicated as the contents of a simple invitation. Hence an exchange heated up, positions hardened. To me of course, its remarks were yet another typical example of life as frequently seen through the subjective prism of an ego's short-sighted perspective.

Try as I might, I have never been able to get my ego to see the big picture, or to explain to it the dangers of instant gratification. Let me tell you, I have gone that extra mile. I have tried to instill the need for the exercise of discipline. I am constantly reminding it that the pursuit of wisdom and knowledge occasionally requires the postponement of pleasure. How many times have I pointed out that snap judgments are not good substitutes for logic and reason? How many times have I preached, "Leave room in your worldview for balance, tolerance, respect for differing opinions," especially those of well-intended human beings blessed with egos that are moderate and reasonable? All to no avail! More than once I have even entertained the possibility of us, my ego and me, going our separate ways. A fantasy, yes. But I have given

it thought—the separation of the ego from the self. What a liberating experience that would be! Imagine, no more petty concerns. No more need of approval from people you don't even like. No more burning desire to be thought of, by everybody, as terrific.

Honest, generous, cool, hot, a winner, a go-getter, on the way to the top—who the hell cares? Who the hell gives a hoot? I say to my ego, "Look, ego, for better or worse it seems we're in this thing together, right? For the long haul, right? Well, shouldn't we try starting off with a little more give-and-take between us? Cut each other a little slack, for goodness' sake. Because when it all boils down, all that's left is just me and you, right? So, if you and me can look at each other through the eye of our mind and see one another as pretty terrific, then it's pretty likely others will see in us what we see in our-selves. Honest, generous, cool—seen by us in such proportions as they do exist through the eye of our own mind, will be visible to those who take the time to look. To the degree that we are hot, a winner, a go-getter, on the way to the top is the degree to which we, you and me, observe, acknowledge, and accept those qualities as a part of our internal selves. Only to that degree will others be able to see us from the inside out. In our completeness, our wholeness.

Still, the reality is, I am inextricably bound to an ego that behaves as if it was breastfed by the pleasure principle. Nevertheless, had I taken pause I might have spotted the imbalance in what otherwise appeared to be a perfect invitation.

But not until I arrived here and had engaged in a mix of casual conversations with some faculty, administrators, and students did I realize that "Come visit and say a few words" really meant more than met the eye. In fact, the phrase was reminiscent of public relations shorthand, which, when translated into full dress, would read more like: "Come visit and say a few hundred thousand words about education. Our expectation is to have the full range of that historically complex question explored by a visiting celebrity personage of your fame and stature who, in our view, also possesses a relatively well-known household name and life experiences of a sort that can sometimes prove vital to American education at certain levels. Therefore, it would be our great pleasure to receive you." That, suddenly, was the moment at which I got nervous. As quick as that, I saw the big picture. I was on thin ice. My ego, on the other hand, being naturally self-absorbed, couldn't see beyond the shorthand version and was still reveling in the moment, preening like a peacock, rhapsodizing in the joy of accomplishment. Obviously, we—it and me—as I am sure you've noticed by now, don't always see eye to eye. Panic signals in my gut went on standby alert, nightmare scenarios began

A publicity shot from the 1970s

creeping into my mind. What if the full-dress version turns out to be the real deal? What would I say, what could I say, about education? I'm short on wisdom and therefore cannot give you absolutes. I'm long on experience, can only give you views, opinions, and maybe a few examples that occasionally might, just might, stand the test of time. Otherwise, I have acquired little in that regard, over and above a few obvious basic truths on which I have relied my whole life long.

A sure sign of humility, I once was told, is when one knows for certain when one is in over one's head. I'm reminded of a saying from the old folks of my youth: "A phrase weighing less than a feather can carry much more than a ton of expectations." This afternoon I began wondering, where did the wires between the invitation and the acceptance get crossed? Why wasn't I paying attention? Finally, somewhere in the last half hour it dawned on me that maybe I am here because of a clerical error and your intent was to invite Harry Belafonte or Bill Cosby. Because there is something wrong with this picture. Me speaking to you! About education! I come with no credentials. In fact, I am the last person you should be listening to on this absolutely major, essential, critical, national issue. It is highly unlikely that your expectations will find much affinity or common ground with whatever views, comments, or perceptions I might offer.

Truth be told, a reversal of our positions would be more appropriate and definitely more productive. You should be standing up here educating me about education, and I should be sitting down there where you are. Right in the middle by myself, listening to your life's experiences. But that right away presents a problem of logistics. All of you up here where I am and me sitting down there where you are, right in the middle by myself. On second thought, there is something wrong with that picture, too. While I would benefit greatly from your collective wisdom, I think we'll have a problem squeezing all of you up here on this little stage. So, it seems we have to stick with the program—clerical error or not. Cosby and Belafonte will have to take a rain check. I am here, unintentionally or not, and you will just have to put up with it.

So now to education—as seen through the eyes of an unevenly educated person. Which is to say that my formal education was not extensive in either time or depth. Therefore, in order that you not be misled by any indications to the contrary, let me state here and now that, for the most part, a haphazard collection of random life experiences were as close as I ever got to a formal education. Yet, while there are no diplomas to be earned from the lessons of life, there's strength to be had for the living of life. Strength of spirit, strength of heart, strength of soul. From my life's experiences, I can tell you: each will be called upon on any journey through this big world. The most profound truth I have stumbled upon in all my wanderings across seventy-four years is a formal in-depth education is the most important tool one can possess in any culture, in any country, in any corner of this twentieth-century world.

To further support that point, I would like to draw your attention to a few obvious, basic truths that relate not just to the subject that is our focus this evening—education—but they are also inextricably intertwined with life itself, in vital and indispensable ways. Unlike profound truths that are said to arrive without notice, illuminate dark and troubled corners of our minds, and leave us changed forever by indelible insights and higher knowledge, obvious basic truths, on the other hand, must vie constantly for our attention by dancing about in the darkness, at the edge of our consciousness. In the meantime, our mind's eye scans the horizon hoping to catch sight of a profound truth heading our way, bringing peace, understanding, and maybe a touch of wisdom, coming to deposit light into the darkest and most troubled corners of our self-awareness.

Unfortunately, there are no flight schedules foretelling the arrival of profound truths, or in whose lives they will eventually touch down. Therefore, for some of us, it might well be our fate that profound truths will pass above our heads and never touch down to bring light into those darkened corners where our doubts and demons live; instead, leave us to fashion peace, understanding, and a touch of wisdom out of such obvious, basic truths as are desperately dancing in the darkness. Trying to be noticed. Trying their best to catch our eye.

Well, as luck would have it, here I am with little to offer. Other than a few obvious, basic truths that have finally caught my eye—some of them as recently as this afternoon.

Here we are! Those words exemplify an "obvious, basic truth." You sitting there in anticipation of what I might have to say and me standing here hoping to impress you with such views and opinions as I might offer in the course of such remarks as I may make on the issue of education, the subject around which we have gathered here tonight. All are obvious, basic truths orbiting our existence, their message waiting to touch down on our behalf whenever we are ready to acknowledge their counsel and receive their judgment. They know more about us than we know of ourselves. They can tell us where we are in life better than any compass could. They can remind us of whether we are standing on the plus or minus side of common ground. And if we are not afraid to take a close hard look, they will even show us who we really are and point the way to what we really can be. The presence of obvious, basic truths also keeps us focused, keeps us from getting too big for our britches, keeps us in touch with the big, challenging, modern, technologically complex world that surrounds us, in which—year by year—our survival needs require us to move faster and faster to simply stay abreast of it.

From obvious, basic truths we have learned that the amount of information necessary to get us through a single day is enormous and growing more so by the hour. We have also learned from obvious, basic truths that some things never change.

Behind the camera for *Uptown Saturday Night* (1974)

Our beginning, yours and mine, is founded still on mysteries locked away still in one or another of nature's unfathomable secrets or buried at the heart of an unalter-able fact. We each, you and I, like all who came before us, emerged out of an ages-old primal process: the fertilization of the egg of a mother by the sperm of a father. Thus, the creation of every human being—generation after generation, from the beginning of the family of man—was ignited by that simple, timeless ritual, which itself is an obvious, basic truth that has not changed. We arrived, with no clue as to what mysteries unfolded on the journey that transformed each of us from a fertilized egg to the little persons that we were at our moment of entry into this big, new, challenging world. No clue as to who we were, what we were, or why we were. Or where we came from. Or what was this new environment into which we had just been born. We knew nothing because conscious recollection had not yet taken root. We hadn't a clue. All we had was a vague undeveloped sense of awareness that we had just been expelled from somewhere that was pretty damn nice.

It therefore could maybe have been argued that a faint and very mild impulse was trying to remind us that we were hooked up to a very comfortable system, wherein everything was automatic: food, sleep, even a little exercise. A feeling that we were housed in a place where all the basic necessities were delivered on demand through a tube that was attached right here. And it seemed the most that was required of us to do was to just lie there in an upside-down position, in that cozy place, kick back, and cool it forever. No clue, no warning, no sensation, and no instinctual notification of any kind that we were getting too big for the space. And that at the end of nine months, if we don't vacate voluntarily, we will be squeezed out or pushed out. That

is the unchanging process by which each generation is obliged to enter this new place with no knowledge, no information, and no experience. Each of which eventually, given time, will show up in the form of obvious, basic truths.

In the meantime, it appears the law of nature mandates that our existence begins with a perfectly clean slate. Primal memory as a factor won't start kicking in for years to come. It may well be that wisp of an impulse which grew to be a survival instinct was but one of many kinds of impulses, fed and nurtured into many kinds of instincts, by a wellspring of primal memories that never break the surface of our consciousness but nonetheless send instincts and impulses across the threshold of human consciousness, through the passageways of our ancestral blood, to inform our lives. Encourage us to be unafraid of the unknown, of love, of forgiveness, to caution us against the indulgence of self, to arm us with second thoughts, to warn us when signs of danger are posted up ahead. So there we were—too weak, or too new, or too unformed, or too traumatized to register a single complaint. And heaven knows we had to have had good and sound reasons for more than a few, considering the fact that we were dispossessed on such short notice from that cool place! Then, in a minute or two, they cut our life supply line. We hadn't been here five minutes, they take a pair of scissors and snip it off. Then they cleaned us up a little bit to get the goop out of our eyes, our noses, our mouths, making it possible for us to take our first-ever look around this new place. Needless to say, somebody had to hold our heads up for us to do that. Truth be told, we didn't know what was waiting for us out here. Coming as we have out of a serene, quiet state of semidarkness, if we did have a clue as to what we would find, we would have fought for an extension to those nine months, to better prepare ourselves for what was symbolized in that first-ever look around this new place. Let me refresh your "impulse"—a bright, blinding light was the first thing that met the eyes. Remember? Of course you don't!

Then, slowly, things of various shapes and sizes started coming into focus—faces, voices, other sounds, other objects—all of which were seen and heard, but none of which made any sense to us. Not even was there the slightest frame of reference to anything we experienced back in that cozy place from which we were forced to take our leave. Pushed out, to put it more to the point.

We came into this new place, this big, challenging world, with no familiarity, no comprehension, no understanding. All we entered with was a tiny bundle of embryonic instincts, which included a fragile amount of sensate awareness and a very little presence of native curiosity about anything above food and sleep, which was automatically guaranteed for nine months—before, of course, the plug was pulled. And furthermore, at that critical stage we don't even have the requisite amount of curiosity to figure all this stuff out. So, we just kind of looked around at all those weird sights that didn't make any sense to us. We saw faces and wondered, "What the hell were those?" And the sounds coming out of those faces. "Hello! Coochie-coochie-coochie." "You look just like your father, yes you do." "Isn't he the cutest thing you ever saw?" "You're going to be spoiled to death, yes you are." Remember? Of course you don't! We just stared at them, not understanding any of that mumbo-jumbo. And how the wisp of an impulse which will, in later life, grow strong and sturdy and be called a "survival instinct" perhaps tried unsuccessfully to alert us on how we could get back to that cozy place we think we just came out of. Perhaps memory, too, was no more than a faint, subtle impulse, and now, once grown, cannot find its way back to its beginning. Could it be that neither an obvious, basic truth nor a profound truth can validate their existence in this big, new, challenging, technologically complex world without the presence of the other? Not unlike the ego and the self!

We wouldn't find out for years that it was our mothers and fathers—with the egg and the sperm business—that had gotten us into this mess in the first place, causing us to wind up in this big, challenging world.

In the meantime, education begins. The learning process was set in motion the moment we arrived—a feel, a touch, a smile. All we would eventually learn would have started out from that first one-on-one between mother and child. Slowly the circle widened, as familiarity and repetition began to weave patterns of interactions, each of which would be captured and reinforced as memory grew stronger.

Sounds and body language send messages to infants as to what to expect. A smile, a kiss, a hug repeated often enough signals to a child that a zone of safety, warmth, protection, and caring is being woven around them. I've been there. So have each of you. Now I am at the other end of the spectrum, where such faint and fading recollections grow dimmer by the day. I now know that we were never meant to find our way back to that cozy place from which we were once expelled and that the true purpose of those recollections was meant merely to help us fix ourselves in time, while dancing in the darkness at the edge of human consciousness with our eyes, our survival instinct, and our remaining hopes and dreams focused on the horizon. Beyond which lies what we assume to be the endless, timeless, and unfathomable dimensions of a region we call the unknown. Out of which, hopefully, will come a profound truth, bearing a touch of wisdom. And will touch down in what remain of our lives, kiss us on our cheeks, and leave us with light enough in the darkened corners of our existence for us to come upon a final understanding of the journey we have made. So that we may then look back and say, "Ahh, there is where I came from—that is who I was—there, in the eyes of the child I used to be, was the purpose of my life's intent—however short I may have fallen—however far afield I may have wandered during a journey held together, across the years, by a few obvious, basic truths. That is who I was. And this is who I am. No more, no less."

Thank you for the invitation.

WEDDING TOAST FOR SYDNEY TAMIIA POITIER

In June 2012, Sidney's youngest daughter, actress Sydney Tamiia Poitier, married composer and music producer Dorian Heartsong at the Church Estate Vineyards in Malibu. These were Sidney's fatherly words on that special occasion.

First—may I say, to you, my daughter, Sydney Tamiia Poitier Heartsong— this evening, for me, is a most extraordinary moment in time. I have been honored by nature and blessed by time to be present here, this afternoon, in the presence of your mother, your sisters, and your many friends, and the many friends of your mother's and mine—and of course, the family members of your husband, Dorian Heartsong, and the attendant members of his family, each of whom is welcomed into open arms.

The journey has begun. The pathways that will beckon you await your arrival. They will lead you across rivers and over mountains. You will see and remember rainbows. You will see reflections of yourselves in the eyes of others. You will listen to the wind, and sometimes you will come to understand its whisperings. I am proud of your efforts to captain your own ship, as difficult as it sometimes can be. I am as proud of your sisters as I am proud of you.

> *Change the world as best you can and nurture the planet Earth as best you can—as this is the only home we have, so far, in the onward journey of the human family.*

What I do expect of you, Mr. and Mrs. Heartsong, is to be happy. Change the world as best you can and nurture the planet Earth as best you can—as this is the only home we have, so far, in the onward journey of the human family. Leave the best of yourselves behind you as guiding lights for generations yet to come. And they, in turn, will leave the best of themselves to continue the onward journey of the human family.

Godspeed and lots of love, my children.

ACKNOWLEDGMENTS

From Joanna Poitier

Thanks first to John Malahy for corralling the disparate treasures of our family archive. To my literary agent, Cait Hoyt; to our editor, Cindy Sipala; to Running Press publisher Kristin Kiser; and the entire Marketing & Publicity team at Running Press, including Seta Zink, Amy Cianfrone, and Betsy Hulsebosch.

From John Malahy

Thanks must first go to Joanna Poitier, who entrusted me with a project so filled with personal meaning. Joanna, I am honored to have helped sustain Sidney's legacy and pleased to have gotten to know you.

At Running Press, thanks to Cindy Sipala for believing I could take on this project and to Randall Lotowycz for helping shepherd me through its development. Thank you also to production editor Melanie Gold and designer Susan Van Horn.

As in all areas of life, I depend on friends and loved ones to get me through. Eli Arnold, Sharon Thackston, Timo Weidner, Tabea Höcker—you are my constant supporters, energizers, and advisers. To craft something like this, one needs a good head on one's shoulders, and that's what my family—Malahy, Arnold, and otherwise—has given me.

Sidney taught me much through this deep dive into his philosophy and values—gratitude for one's family, the importance of lifelong friendships, the wisdom of one's elders, the centrality of education and self-betterment. His words will stay with me forever.

INDEX

Images are in BOLD.